CONTENTS

CONTENTS

INTRODUCTION

I was a little apprehensive when I moved to Kansas to become the *Wichita Eagle*'s food editor in late 1999. Would a landlocked city in a culturally conservative state offer much in the way of variety?

It took me about a week to realize that Wichita boasted more food diversity than any similarly sized city I'd ever visited—and more than many bigger cities as well. In particular, Asian, Hispanic and Mediterranean restaurants and markets were plentiful, serving immigrant populations and adventurous natives alike. Good American cooking and the food of other cultures were represented, too, in settings ranging from white-cloth restaurants and church gymnasiums to corner bars and backyard grills.

Since then, the situation has only improved. Like most of the country, Wichita benefited from aspects of the foodie revolution: the farm-to-table movement, chef-driven menus, food trucks, microbreweries and coffeehouses. We can be grateful that a few others—molecular gastronomy, anyone?—never took hold here.

I recall one other concern prior to arriving: Would Wichitans be willing to share their knowledge of cooking with someone they hardly knew?

It turns out that the city's cooks were a lot more willing to share than the politicians, cops and crooks I'd spent the earlier part of my journalism career covering. "There are no secrets in cooking," Tanya Tandoc, the owner of Tanya's Soup Kitchen, told me during our first meeting. (That was easy for her to say, as she had an uncanny ability to take the tiniest taste of a dish and discern exactly what was in it.)

Domitilla Yu, a member of the Sisters of St. Joseph, prepares food from her native Korea as the author looks on. Yu's recipes for Korean barbecue and egg rolls appear in chapter 6. *Photo by Jaime Green/Wichita Eagle.*

Other chefs and restaurant owners were just as welcoming. Ty Issa, whose Larkspur restaurant sits across the street from the *Eagle*'s former location on Douglas Avenue, offered me the use of its kitchen and ingredients whenever I needed them. Melad Stephan of Sabor (and Oeno, Egg Cetera and others before that) showed me many kitchen tricks and techniques I use regularly in my cooking classes and entertaining. And one chef, Danny Nguyen of Pho Hot Bistro and Lemongrass, became a close friend while giving me a years-long master's class in Vietnamese cooking.

Home cooks also eagerly shared their recipes and tips. In many cases, these amateurs brought passion and skills to the kitchen that surpassed the pros.

I've now been writing about food in Wichita for more than twenty years, first for the *Eagle*, then for *Splurge* magazine and *The Active Age*. That adds up to around seven hundred articles and columns. I want to thank all three publications for permission to use material that appeared in them previously. Even more, I want to thank my wife, editor and chief taste-tester, Carrie.

I hope you find this book entertaining and useful. My wish is that it becomes splattered with extra-virgin olive oil and encrusted in kosher salt by the time you're done with it. Many of the recipes are simple, and most can be prepared with ingredients found in the supermarket. For those that require a trip to one of our city's ethnic markets, you're in for a fun adventure if you've never been. Recipes marked with an asterisk are ones I've made over and over.

I've done my best to accurately reproduce the recipes given to me by local cooks. Any errors are undoubtedly my own. Cooking is a personal undertaking, so please adjust recipes as you see fit. With the exception of baking, which demands some exactitude, most recipes can be modified successfully.

This book is not an attempt to tell the complete history of foodways in our city. Rather, it's a personal account of what I've eaten, learned and loved during my time here. It wasn't easy deciding what to put in this book, and I've had to leave out some of the city's best cooks and recipes, past and present. So to all the great cooks of Wichita—represented here or not—I dedicate this book to you with sincere appreciation.

PART I

BEGINNINGS

Chapter 1

PIONEERING WOMEN

Cooking in early Wichita wasn't a job for wussies. In addition to the necessity of raising or killing much of what went onto their plates, the frontier settlement's cooks had to deal with kitchen equipment that would send many cooks today straight to Uber Eats.

I got a tiny taste of what cooking was like back then one day at Old Cowtown Museum, the living history museum on the banks of the Arkansas River. The occasion was Kansas Day, celebrated each January 29. Then employed as the *Wichita Eagle*'s food editor, I came up with the brilliant idea of tagging along as Mark Shanks, Cowtown's director of historical interpretation, prepared a meal in the museum's circa 1884 farmhouse.

It turned out to be one of the coldest days of the year—fifteen degrees with a blustery wind blowing through the old farmhouse's walls. Shanks and *Eagle* photographer Jaime Green had donned long underwear; I soon wished I had done the same.

The stove was heavy black iron. It took Shanks a box of wood and much of the morning to get the thing hot enough to cook anything. I suppose it could have been worse: In frontier days, when the Kansas prairie was nearly treeless, the fuel used for cooking probably would have been cow chips, adding a distinctive aroma to the occasion. We also would have been forced to pump our water out of a frozen well.

For the coffee, Shanks toasted some green coffee beans in a skillet until they were dark, pulverized them in a hand-cranked grinder and then

Maria Lopez, a historical interpreter at Old Cowtown Museum, cooks on a cast-iron stove in the museum's farmhouse—not as easy as it looks. *Courtesy of Old Cowtown Museum.*

boiled them in a coffee pot fitted with a not-too-efficient strainer. The result was weak, gritty and nearly undrinkable. The oven never got hot enough to bake biscuits. The rest of the dinner—smothered pork chops, mashed turnips and a kind of dried apple tart—was pretty good. Or maybe we were just hungry after standing around the freezing farmhouse all morning.

Of course, most cooking back then was done by women, who also tended home garden plots, collected eggs daily and butchered chickens for Sunday dinner. Because of Kansas's limited growing season, root vegetables that could be stored in a cellar during the winter were crucial to these cooks. Canning—invented less than a century earlier to feed Napoleon Bonaparte's armies—also was on the rise.

The coming of the railroad in 1872—two years after Wichita's founding—opened up more food options for those with money, suddenly making available everything from spices to ice cream and oysters packed on blocks of ice.

THE NATION'S OLDEST COOKING CLUB

As the city grew, homemakers added refined touches to their dinner tables. In 1891, a group of women started the Thursday Afternoon Cooking Club, sharing recipes and cooking techniques with the goal of making sure that younger members knew how to entertain properly. At the first meeting, one member gave a lesson on making homemade mayonnaise, while another prepared oyster patties. The iconic Riverside Castle became a favorite meeting place for the group since one of the group's founders, Mrs. B.H. Campbell, lived there. Through ensuing decades, club menus and minutes show members adjusting to events such as wartime rationing, the rise of convenience foods and health-conscious cooking.

The club still meets today, albeit on a monthly rather than twice-monthly basis. That makes it the oldest such club of its kind in the United States, according to a long, glowing 2015 feature in the *New York Times*. There was talk of turning the article into a movie, but nothing came of it. Apparently, there hadn't been enough intra-club drama through the years.

Fast-forward a century after the Thursday Afternoon Cooking Club's start, and women were still pushing the city's culinary habits forward. None was more recognizable than Kathleen Kelly, who served as the *Eagle*'s food writer from 1955 through 1994. Known for her fancy hats and down-to-

Kathleen Kelly traveled to China, Italy, Scandinavia and other foreign countries as the longtime *Wichita Eagle* food writer. *Courtesy of the* Wichita Eagle.

earth approach, Kelly was in most respects lucky to work during the heyday of the newspaper business. The *Eagle* sent her around the world to learn about food and bring that knowledge home to readers. Only those readers with long memories would remember that Kelly's husband had died in a 1960 plane crash while working as a photographer for the *Eagle*. "People don't know that the *Wichita Eagle* took a husband from me," Kelly said upon retiring.

Throughout the 1990s, one of the hottest tickets in town was a seat at the cooking classes Bonnie Aeschliman taught. Aeschliman, who was head of the home economics department at Heights High School, offered classes in her Bel Aire home, and each of the twenty-five slots filled up as soon as she announced the sessions. Aeschliman taught classes on a wide variety of foods but probably was best known for the kind of simple, delectable recipes she'd learned growing up in Missouri—what she called "rural chic." Aeschliman later opened a cooking store and studio called Cooking at Bonnie's Place before moving to Tennessee to sell real estate.

Downtown, two other women were creating legacies in the field of professional cooking. Pat Brown started washing dishes at the Lassen Hotel in the early 1960s as an African American teenager from tiny Paris, Arkansas. By 1999, she was running the kitchen at the private Petroleum Club, located on the ninth floor of what's now the Ruffin Building. Along the way, she helped chefs across the city make the same kind of journey in their careers. Many viewed the sixty-something Brown as a second mother.

Colette Baptista, head of the food service program at Wichita Area Technical College (WATC), was churning out cooks from the basement of the old Wichita High School on Emporia. Like Brown, Baptista had played a big, if mostly behind-the-scenes, role in the city's food scene during her twenty-four years at the school. This was before the foodie revolution fully arrived in Wichita, and WATC shut down the program (although its successor, WSU Tech, is now developing a new downtown cooking school). Baptista went on to run a successful catering business.

Colette Baptista trained chefs at Wichita Area Technical College for many years.

Meanwhile, in north Wichita, Pat Randleas gave up her day job to raise produce with the help of her husband, Elzie, and various family and friends on a property that can only be described as eclectic. Pat, who drives an old pickup around delivering these delicacies to the back doors of restaurants, also built the Old Town Farmers Market into a Saturday morning institution after a falling-out with the Kansas Grown Farmers Market at 21st and Ridge Road. While Pat can be opinionated and politically incorrect (in her own words), I appreciate her humor and candor, and she indisputably played a big part in helping the "Eat Local" movement take off here. She gave up running the Old Town market a few years ago but still is raising and selling great food.

Of course, there were many other people, both men and women, doing great things with food. These were just a few I met soon after moving here—enough to convince me I was going to like it just fine.

Strawberry Romaine Salad

This recipe comes from *Thursday Afternoon Cooking Club* by Sondra Langel, one of several cookbooks featuring the club's recipes that have been published during its long history.

Source: *Thursday Afternoon Cooking Club* (2018) by Sondra Langel

Dressing:
2 cups mayonnaise
⅓ cup sugar
⅓ cup light cream
⅓ cup raspberry vinegar
2 tablespoons poppy seed
2–3 teaspoons raspberry jam

1 head romaine lettuce, washed and torn
1 pint fresh strawberries, sliced
1 red onion, sliced
¼ cup slivered almonds, toasted

Combine dressing ingredients; set aside. Toss romaine, strawberries and onion. Just before serving, drizzle dressing over salad. Garnish with almonds.

Orange Glazed Baked Ham
Source: Bonnie Aeschliman

1 (8- to 10-pound) smoked, fully cooked bone-in, half ham

Glaze:
½ cup orange marmalade
¼ cup Dijon mustard
¼ cup brown sugar

Garnish:
Fresh lemon leaves or parsley
Orange slices

Position rack in center of oven and preheat to 325 degrees. Place ham in a roasting pan and cook according to package directions.

Meanwhile, bring orange marmalade, mustard and brown sugar to a boil in a small saucepan. Set aside.

Thirty minutes before ham is done, remove from oven and brush with glaze. Return to oven to finish cooking and for glaze to set and begin to caramelize. Let ham stand 30 minutes before slicing. Garnish with lemon leaves or parsley and orange slices.

Note: Be sure to use a good-quality ham. The label should read ''ham and natural juices'' rather than ''ham and water product.''

Creamed New Potatoes and Peas
Source: Bonnie Aeschliman

2 pounds small new red potatoes
½ teaspoon salt
1 bag (16 ounces) frozen baby peas
1 teaspoon sugar (optional)
¾ to 1 cup heavy cream
Salt and freshly ground black pepper, to taste

Scrub new potatoes. Peel a strip from around the equator of each potato. Place potato, 1 cup water and ½ teaspoon salt in a large saucepan. Bring to a boil. Reduce heat, cover and simmer until tender, about 20 minutes.

Add frozen peas and sugar to potatoes; cover and cook for 3 to 4 minutes. There will not be much liquid left in the pan. Remove lid and cook a few minutes to evaporate most of the liquid.

Add cream. Simmer uncovered a few minutes until cream is thickened to sauce consistency. Season to taste with salt and freshly ground black pepper.

Banana Cream Pie
Source: Pat Brown

3 cups half-and-half
½ cup sugar
¼ cup cornstarch
4 egg yolks
2 ripe bananas, sliced
1 ½ teaspoons vanilla
1 pie crust
Whipped topping
Sliced almonds

In a large saucepan, combine half-and-half, sugar and cornstarch. Cook over medium-low heat until mixture begins to boil and thicken, about 20 minutes, stirring occasionally to keep bottom from burning.

In the meantime, beat egg yolks slightly in a separate bowl. Temper egg yolks by stirring about 1 cup of hot mixture into them and then pouring the combination back into the saucepan. Return to bowl, then remove from heat and stir in sliced bananas and vanilla.

Let cool while baking empty pie crust for 10 minutes at 325 degrees. Let pie shell cool, then pour filling into it and refrigerate.

Before serving, top with whipped topping and almonds.

Mama's Spice Cake
Longtime culinary instructor Colette Baptista learned this recipe from her mother as a child. It remains a favorite.

2 cups brown sugar
½ cup butter, softened
3 eggs
1 cup sour cream
1 cup buttermilk (or 1 tablespoon lemon juice or vinegar mixed with enough milk to make 1 cup)
1 tablespoon baking soda
1 teaspoon baking powder
1 tablespoon cinnamon

1 teaspoon ground cloves
½ teaspoon nutmeg
3 cups flour

Cream sugar and butter together until light and fluffy. Beat in eggs one at a time. Combine sour cream, buttermilk and baking soda in a bowl. Stir into sugar-butter-egg mixture. Stir or sift together baking powder, cinnamon, cloves, nutmeg and flour in a separate bowl. Dump dry ingredients into wet mixture, stirring until just combined.

Pour batter into a lightly greased 9x13-inch baking pan. Bake in a preheated 350-degree oven for 45 minutes to 1 hour, or until a tester comes out dry.

Farmers Market Frittata
Source: Pat Randleas

Olive oil
3 to 4 cups fresh spinach leaves, torn or roughly chopped
2 to 3 scallions, chopped
¼ pound asparagus stalks, tough ends trimmed
8 to 10 eggs
Dash milk
Salt and pepper
1 cup feta cheese

Pat Randleas sold food for a restaurant supply company before deciding to start growing and selling her own produce.

Heat oil in 10-inch skillet over medium-high heat. Add spinach leaves and scallions and cook until spinach is wilted. Remove skillet from heat. Cook asparagus in a pot of boiling, salted water about 2 to 3 minutes or until crisp tender. Drain, cool slightly and chop into 1-inch pieces. Add asparagus to skillet.

Preheat oven to 400 degrees. Return skillet to stovetop burner. Beat eggs with milk, salt and pepper. Pour egg mixture over vegetables, adding oil to skillet if it appears dry. Cook eggs over medium heat until the edges begin to set. (Loosening edges with a spatula will make it easier to get out of the skillet later.) Sprinkle frittata with cheese. Transfer skillet to oven to finish cooking, about 10 to 12 minutes or until done.

Chapter 2

SALAD DAYS

All during my time at the *Wichita Eagle*, people begged me for the garlic salad recipe from Doc's Steakhouse on North Broadway. The funny thing is, the recipe was available—to anyone willing to pay $700,000 for it. That's the price then-owner Stuart Scott put on his secret formula for the concoction. I think he was willing to throw in the restaurant, too.

The salad was unusual: Although it contained lettuce, it was a dip or spread you ate with crackers rather than a salad in the traditional sense. In fact, it was so loaded with mayonnaise and garlic salt that spooning it down straight would have been a struggle. But that it was popular, there's no doubt.

Doc's closed in the early 2000s, reopened at least twice and now appears to have shut its doors for good. At one time, it was one of at least four restaurants—three of them serving their own version of garlic salad—that helped make the North Broadway area Wichita's prime entertainment destination. The others were Abe's Steakhouse, Ken's Klub and Savute's Italian Ristorante. Only Savute's remains in business. (Wichita's chain of NuWay sandwich shops has garlic salad on the menu, but aficionados say it's not the steakhouse version.)

Eventually summoning my inner investigative journalist (and lacking $700,000), I decided to try to uncover the secret of garlic salad. By then, I also was interested in whether the dish originated in Wichita, since I'd never seen it served anywhere else.

Even a top-secret recipe for garlic salad couldn't keep Doc's Steakhouse on North Broadway open forever.

Scott told me he didn't know where the recipe came from. It was part of the deal when his family bought the restaurant from Dwight "Doc" Hustead in 1963. But Scott provided a clue by mentioning that Hustead had worked for another establishment—Ken's Klub—before opening his own.

Its owner, Ken Hill, died in 1998, but I was able to get in touch with his daughter, Suzy Hill, who filled me in on her colorful father. Once a ranked welterweight fighter, Ken Hill started his restaurant in 1946 after serving as an infantry captain in Europe during World War II. Hill opened his place just north of what was then the city limits, on the spot where Cortez Mexican Restaurant later operated for many years.

FROM K-RATIONS TO KEN'S KLUB

Ken's Klub was the kind of place Wichitans took visiting friends and celebrities to eat. The owner liked to hand out cigars and once served an overflow New Year's Eve crowd in his own house next door. When parties lasted until dawn, Hill whipped up breakfast. But people also knew better than to get out of line with the ex-boxer.

Hill made food soldiers had fantasized about while surviving on K-rations—food like steak, fried chicken, onion rings and even deep-fried steak tips. According to his daughter, Hill threw together the garlic salad one night during a dinner rush when the restaurant ran out of its regular bottled salad dressing. Suzy Hill said there were several keys to getting it just right: Ken's used only Hellmann's mayonnaise, lettuce bought that day and the Schilling brand (now McCormick) of garlic salt. Outer leaves of lettuce were removed (to be used to line the bowl the salad was served in), the core was discarded and the leaves were chopped into nickel- or dime-size pieces (not as small as the cabbage in coleslaw). The lettuce was then squeezed and drained to draw out moisture so that it would stay crisp. A bit of chopped carrot and radish was mixed in, and the combination was kept cold. The dressing was added just before serving, and the salad was garnished with a stem of parsley, a rosebud radish and crackers.

When Suzy prepared this version for me in her Riverside home, I had to admit it was pretty addictive.

Now I knew how to make the salad, but I still wondered if Ken Hill really was the inventor. I looked through old cookbooks and came up empty. I phoned the people who stage the world's largest garlic festival, in Gilroy, California, and asked if they'd seen such a dish. They said no. I Googled "garlic salad" and found nothing like it (okay, I didn't look at all 615,000 items featuring those two words).

Finally, I wondered if it could have originated in Lebanon, a country that likes its garlic, since the owners of Abe's Steakhouse were of Lebanese descent. I talked to Tony Abdayem, the former owner of La Galette, who briefly revived Abe's Steakhouse in the early 2000s.

"We eat a lot of garlic [in Lebanon], but we don't have anything like that at home," Abdayem said.

And with that, I was ready to crown Ken Hill the garlic salad champion of the world.

Ken's Klub's Garlic Salad
Source: Suzy Hill

1 cup Hellmann's mayonnaise
1–2 teaspoons McCormick garlic salt
2 tablespoons tomato juice
1 head lettuce
1 cup grated carrot and radish

Garnish: sprig parsley, radish roses, paprika
Crackers (Club or Ritz are recommended)

Mix mayonnaise, garlic salt and tomato juice. Refrigerate.

Remove outer leaves and core from head of lettuce (outer leaves can be washed, drained and used to line salad plate or bowl).

Chop remaining lettuce into dime-size pieces to fill 6 cups. Line a colander with paper towels, place lettuce in colander and top with more paper towels. Press down on lettuce to extract moisture. Remove lettuce from colander and place in plastic bag lined with more paper towels. Refrigerate several hours. Grate carrots and radishes and pat dry. Refrigerate.

Just before serving, toss chopped vegetables with dressing. Mound salad in bowl or plate and garnish with parsley, radish rose and paprika. Serve with crackers.

PART II

THREE GREAT CUISINES

Chapter 3

MIDDLE EAST MEETS MIDDLE WEST

Here's some food for thought: if not for three villages in southern Lebanon, the culinary scene in Wichita would look and taste a whole lot different than it does today.

Imagine no annual Lebanese dinners drawing thousands of fans to the city's Orthodox churches for kibbeh and cabbage rolls. No fresh-baked pita and baklava readily available any time of year. And a significant percentage of the city's best-known restaurants either nonexistent or in other hands.

In other words, not a culinary landscape I want to inhabit.

The first Lebanese immigrants arrived here in the late 1800s and early 1900s, prompted to leave their homeland, then part of Syria, for religious, political and economic reasons. Most came from three small towns in southern Lebanon: Ain Arab, Mhaite and Jdeidet Marjeyoun. From Ain Arab came the Kallail, Laham and Solomon families; from Mhaite, a short walk away, came the Steven, Namee, Wolf and Ferris families; and from Jdeidet Marjeyoun, about twenty miles distant, came the Farha, Cohlmia, Bayouth, Ojile and Shadid families. (The author is indebted to *Wichita's Lebanese Heritage*, published by The History Press in 2010 and written by Jay Price, Victoria Sherry and Matthew Namee, for this background.)

Some of the immigrants became peddlers, selling lace, housewares and other goods from horse-drawn buggies in the Kansas countryside until they could save enough money to open businesses in Wichita. When they did, food often became a focus.

Melad Stephan, a native of Lebanon and the owner of Sabor in Old Town Square, often feeds actor Harrison Ford when the aviation enthusiast comes to Wichita. Stephan's wife, Deanna, is shown between the men. *Courtesy of Melad Stephan.*

The Farhas and Elkouris started in the restaurant supply business with F&E Wholesale Groceries, as did the Ablahs with Ablah Hotel Supply Co. Members of the Bayouth, Kallail, Stephan, Shadid, Elkouri, Wolf, Farha and Ablah families ran groceries; the Farha and Ablah clans developed theirs into chains. A few opened restaurants and nightclubs, such as the Abrahams' Abe's Steakhouse, the Steven family's Plamor and Hi Ho clubs and the Ferrises' Freddie's Brass Rail.

Those of the Orthodox Christian faith founded two churches, St. George and St. Mary (both originally in the Delano neighborhood), which is where many Wichitans first tasted authentic Lebanese food. St. George's annual dinner, which stretches over two days and feeds upward of six thousand people, dates to 1921. The St. Mary dinner is smaller and nearly as old.

ST. GEORGE AND SPANGLES

Lebanese food draws on influences from the Middle East, southern Europe and northern Africa. Olive oil is a major flavoring ingredient and not just the preferred cooking fat; garlic, fresh herbs and dried spices, nuts and citrus fruits play big roles. Communal eating, in the form of dips like hummus and

Brad Steven, pictured, owns the Wine Dive and Vora restaurants with his brother, Brent. They're part of a family that has fed and entertained Wichitans since the 1940s.

baba ganoush scooped up with the flatbread known as pita, is common.

At St. George, it takes volunteers months to plan and prepare the dinner. I spent one day in the church kitchen with four generations of Kouris and Elkouris. The work is meticulous, from clarifying butter for baklava to trimming every bit of fat and sinew from sirloin for kibbeh. In the old days, before the phyllo dough used for baklava became commercially available, parishioners stood around a big table stretching and pulling it by hand until it was paper thin. That must have been something to see.

The Steven family, part of a smaller contingent of Roman Catholic immigrants from Lebanon, also put a major stamp on our city's culinary landscape. Dale, Craig and Rene Steven built the Spangles fast-food chain, which has sixteen locations in the Wichita area as of this writing. A younger generation has gravitated to upscale eateries—Brandon Steven's 6S Steakhouse and his cousins Brad and Brent Steven's Vora and Wine Dive.

AN OLIVE TREE WITH MANY BRANCHES

A new wave of Lebanese influence in Wichita began in 1973 when Antoine Toubia moved here to become chef at Crestview Country Club. A native of Beirut (his family originally came from near Jdeidet Marjeyoun), Toubia cooked in New York and Kansas City prior to his arrival. In 1979, joined by his parents and several siblings, he opened his first Olive Tree restaurant at Kellogg and Oliver.

The restaurant was a hit, and not just because it made Middle Eastern staples such as hummus and tabbouleh available on a regular basis. Toubia's cooking was strongly influenced by French cuisine—Beirut once was known as the "Paris of the Middle East—and so included unfamiliar dishes such as fresh salmon and lamb, crepes and quiche, elegant pastries and exotic accompaniments such as *au poivre* (peppercorn sauce). Good wine was an essential part of the experience, a full generation before many Americans

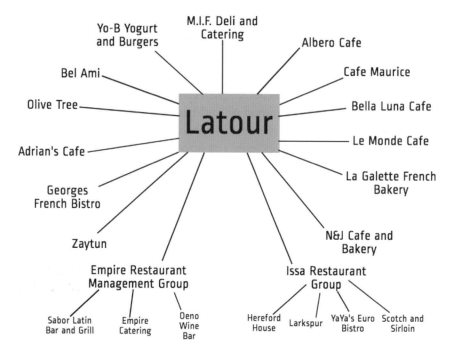

A chart shows restaurants and catering operations opened by former employees of Latour. *Courtesy of KMUW.*

had drunk anything more adventurous than chardonnay. Underlying it all was an ethos of dining as an unhurried, celebratory event, with service as smooth as a drizzle of olive oil.

The Toubia family's food empire, Latour Management (named for a type of grape), grew to include past and present favorites Bagatelle Bakery, Café Chantilly, Chelsea's and Piccadilly market and deli, along with a number of food service contracts. At one time, it employed 450 people, although it's now considerably smaller. Dozens of the city's most prominent chefs and restaurant owners worked for Latour before going on to start their own restaurants.

STEAKS AND PANCAKES

Lebanon's later turmoil—a civil war raged from 1975 to 1990—spurred still more immigration to Wichita. Melad Stephan, a relative of the Steven family, made the move in the late 1970s. He worked for the Stevens and Latour before opening a string of restaurants that heralded the Old Town entertainment district's redevelopment: Uptown Bistro, Oeno Wine Bar, Egg Cetera and currently Sabor Latin Bar & Grille.

Ty Issa, who owns Scotch & Sirloin, Larkspur and YaYa's with his brothers Mike and Ali, came here to study engineering at Wichita State University before deciding that upscale dining was his destined field. The brothers also own an IHOP franchise.

The lure of WSU and continuing disorder in Lebanon brought Alex Harb to Wichita, where he cooked and waited tables to put himself through college. After building a successful computer business, Harb launched the fast-casual Meddy's chain with aspirations of taking it nationwide.

The Lebanese influence in Wichita food circles shows no sign of abating, even when the food is far removed from its origin. Patrick Shibley, the chef behind the gourmet comfort food at Doo-Dah Diner, is half Lebanese; his dad, Kamiel, owned and ran restaurants here for forty years.

George Youssef, who emigrated from Lebanon via Canada, created a stir in 2015 when he opened Georges French Bistro, the type of brassiere one might find in Montreal or Paris. More recently, he and a partner took over one of the city's swankiest steakhouses, Chester's Chophouse & Wine Bar. There's not a stuffed grape leaf or plate of hummus to be found on either menu.

Beef shawarma served atop hummus at Meddys, a Mediterranean restaurant with several locations. "People in Wichita eat more hummus than in all of Lebanon," one restaurant owner who's from that country joked.

*Grilled Sweet Peppers

Melad Stephan's Oeno Wine Bar in Old Town Square often featured
a complimentary table of mezze, or appetizers. Prettiest of all were
the small, sweet, multicolored peppers now widely available in
supermarkets, transformed with nothing more than olive oil, garlic, salt,
pepper and heat.
Source: Melad Stephan

1 bag small, sweet, multicolored peppers
Minced garlic
Olive oil
Salt and pepper

Toss peppers, garlic, olive oil, salt and pepper in a large bowl. Heat a
skillet over medium-high heat. Grill peppers, turning occasionally, until
they have browned in spots and easily collapse when pressed. Pile on
plate and serve warm or at room temperature.

Note: Leftover peppers can be incorporated into omelets, pasta
dishes, wraps and more.

*Lavash Pizza

Another favorite from Oeno's mezze platter. Lavash is a large, round
flatbread sold in the deli department of many supermarkets. Before
cooking, its texture is like that of a cracker.
Source: Melad Stephan

1 block (8 ounces) regular or flavored Havarti cheese
1 lavash cracker bread
Olive oil
Roasted garlic cloves (available in some supermarkets, or see directions below)

Preheat oven to 350 degrees.
Slice Havarti cheese as thinly as possible and cover lavash with slices.
Place lavash on cookie sheet or pizza tray that's been greased with
vegetable or olive oil.

Cook lavash about 5 minutes, or just until cheese melts and lavash softens. Remove from oven, slice while hot and serve.

Roasted garlic: To roast garlic, cut the tips off a head of garlic cloves, leaving the head intact. Place the head in a ramekin, drizzle with olive oil and season with salt and pepper. Cover with aluminum foil and bake at 400 degrees about 30 minutes or until cloves are softened and slip easily from their skins.

Former Byblos owner Ilham Saad and two of her five daughters take a break from a cooking demonstration at the annual Women's Fair. All of Saad's daughters grew up working in the restaurant owned by their parents. *Courtesy of Ilham Saad.*

Fattoush Salad

For years, I lived near a Lebanese restaurant and market whose owner, Ilham Saad, was happy to share her expertise. Byblos, although now closed, was the classic American success story, allowing Saad and her husband, Kamal, to raise five beautiful daughters, who worked there as they grew up. Ilham prepared just about every dish that went out to customers while somehow finding time for leisurely conversations with them. In 2019, after many years of work, Saad published her own cookbook, *Cooking with Inspiration* (available at cookingwithinspiration. com and some local stores).

Source: Ilham Saad

2 pita loaves
1 head romaine lettuce
1 head iceberg lettuce
3 tomatoes, chopped
1 bunch green onions, chopped
1 cucumber, sliced
6 radishes, sliced
1 green or red bell pepper, chopped

Dressing:
½ cup lemon juice
½ cup olive oil
Sumac (see notes on ingredients)
Salt, to taste

Bake pita loaves on an ungreased baking sheet in a 350-degree oven about 12 minutes. Remove and cool. Break into chip-size pieces.

Combine pita pieces, lettuce, tomatoes, green onions, cucumber, radishes and bell pepper in large bowl. Sprinkle lemon juice, olive oil, sumac and salt over vegetables. Toss and serve.

Note: Sumac is a tangy Middle Eastern spice. Lemon zest may be substituted.

Chicken Shawarma

N&J Café has turned the corner of Lincoln and Edgemoor into a one-stop shop for fans of Lebanese food. In the same building are the N&J Global Market and John's Bakery, which produces pita bread for N&J and other restaurants; its thin and chewy pita is my personal favorite of all I've tried. (Po Boy Pizza, located across the street and started by another family of Lebanese immigrants, makes a good but much different type of pita.) The sons of the late N&J founder John Srour had just taken over and were planning major upgrades as this was being written.
Source: N&J Cafe

1 pound boneless chicken breasts or thighs

Marinade:
2 tablespoons mustard
2 cloves garlic, minced
⅛ cup chopped onion
½ teaspoon salt
1 tablespoon chopped parsley
1 teaspoon vegetable oil
Pinch each black and white pepper
1 teaspoon lemon juice

Humus:
1 can (15 ounces) garbanzo beans, drained
½ cup water
3 tablespoons tahini (see notes on ingredients)
1 clove garlic, minced
2 tablespoons lemon juice
½ teaspoon salt

Garnish:
½ red onion, chopped
1 tomato, chopped
½ bunch parsley, chopped
Olives
Toasted or regular pita chips

Cut chicken into 1-inch strips. Combine marinade ingredients in nonreactive bowl. Add chicken pieces and stir until pieces are evenly coated. Cover and refrigerate at least 8 hours or overnight.

Meanwhile, prepare humus by placing garbanzo beans, water, tahini and garlic in a food processor or blender and processing until smooth. Add lemon juice and salt.

Heat 1 tablespoon oil in a large sauté pan. Add onion and chicken and cook over medium-high heat until chicken is done, about 5 minutes. Add tomato and parsley during last minute of cooking.

Place chicken mixture in the center of a large serving platter. Surround it with a ring of humus dotted with olives. Serve with toasted or regular pita chips.

Note: Tahini, a paste made of sesame seeds, is sold in many supermarkets.

*Manoushi

Recipes don't come much easier and tastier than this specialty of Bagatelle, the café and bakery on East Harry. Manoushi is like a thin crust pizza you make in minutes. Pita bread freezes well and thaws in 20 seconds in the microwave. Keep a bag in your freezer, and you'll never be without a great snack or meal.
Source: Bagatelle

Olive oil
1 pita loaf
⅓ cup halloumi, feta or mozzarella
1 small tomato, sliced
1 tablespoon freshly chopped herbs, such as oregano, thyme or basil

Preheat oven to 350 degrees. Brush olive oil over pita loaf. Slice cheese into thin pieces and place on pita loaf. Top with tomato and herbs.

Put pita loaf on a lightly oiled baking sheet and bake until cheese melts and edges of pita start to brown, about 5 to 7 minutes. Serve warm or at room temperature.

Beef Manoushi: Brown ¼ pound hamburger in skillet; drain off grease. Season with 1 teaspoon sumac and salt to taste. Brush pita with olive oil. Spread beef over pita and bake 7 minutes. Garnish with sprig of mint.

Za'atar Manoushi: Brush pita loaf with olive oil. Sprinkle 1 tablespoon za'atar (a blend of sesame seeds, dried thyme and sumac). Bake 7 minutes. Serve with side of plain yogurt.

Mediterranean Bean Salad

George Youssef concocted this cool and summery dish while running his first Wichita restaurant, Nouvelle Café, on Rock Road. It's great on its own or served with grilled fish or chicken.
Source: George Youssef

2 cans (about 16 ounces each) large butter or white beans, rinsed and drained
4 garlic cloves, minced
20 cherry tomatoes, halved
Juice of 2 small lemons
¼ cup olive oil
1 teaspoon salt
Freshly ground black pepper, to taste

2 tablespoons fresh mint
2 tablespoons fresh oregano
2 tablespoons fresh thyme

Combine all ingredients in a bowl and refrigerate several hours before serving to allow the flavors to blend.

Kibbeh

This is the Americanized version of kibbeh. In the traditional version, the mixture that makes up the top and bottom layers is served raw on its own, similar to steak tartare, and is considered a celebratory dish.
Source: St. George Orthodox Christian Cathedral

Top and bottom layers (kibbeh):
1 cup bulgur wheat, soaked and drained with all the water squeezed out
1 medium onion, chopped
1 tablespoon salt
1 teaspoon cinnamon
½ teaspoon black pepper
1 tablespoon marjoram
1 pound ground sirloin steak (trimmed of fat and gristle)

Middle layer (hushwa):
1 pound coarsely ground beef
1 medium onion, chopped
1 teaspoon salt
½ teaspoon cinnamon
¼ teaspoon pepper
3 tablespoons clarified butter, divided use
2 tablespoons lemon juice

For top and bottom layers (kibbeh): Wash wheat and drain. Grind onion, then add onion, salt and spices to meat and mix well. Add this mixture to wheat and mix well with hands.

For middle layer (hushwa), cook meat with onion until meat is tender and dry. Add salt, spices, 1 tablespoon butter and lemon juice.

Grease a 1-quart casserole. Take half the kibbeh mixture and pat into the bottom of the pan. Sprinkle with hushwa to form middle layer. Cover hushwa with second half of the kibbeh meat. Dip hand in ice water and smooth top. Cut into squares.

Top with remaining clarified butter and bake for 1 hour at 350 degrees.

Cabbage Rolls
Source: St. George Orthodox Christian Cathedral

Stuffing:
1 cup uncooked rice
2 cups coarsely ground beef
2 tablespoons clarified butter
1 tablespoon salt
1 teaspoon cinnamon
¼ teaspoon pepper

Cabbage:
2 ⅓ tablespoons salt, divided use
1 head cabbage
3 cloves garlic
½ cup lemon juice

Wash and drain rice. Add meat, butter and seasonings and mix well. Set aside.

In a pot with enough water to cover cabbage, add 2 tablespoons salt and bring to boil. Remove core from bottom center of cabbage with a knife. Drop cabbage into boiling water for 3 to 5 minutes, separating cabbage leaves with tongs as it boils.

Remove leaves from water when wilted and place in a pan of ice water until cool enough to handle. Slice off heavy rib on leaves. If leaves are large, cut them in half. Place a heaping tablespoon of rice and meat filling on each cut leaf and roll firmly.

Cover the bottom of a 2- or 3-quart pan with extra pieces of cabbage. (This prevents cabbage rolls from sticking to bottom.) Lay cabbage rolls neatly in rows in the pan, making several layers. Place 3 cloves of garlic among layers.

Place a saucer on top of cabbage rolls for weight. Pour water with 1 teaspoon salt and ½ cup lemon juice over cabbage rolls, enough to barely cover. Bring to a boil. Reduce heat and cook on low for 1 hour.

*Baklava

Baklava is popular around the Middle East and eastern Mediterranean. Here's a recipe drawn from several sources that I've taught to community cooking classes at Mark Arts.

Baklava: Like many Lebanese dishes, the sweet multilayered pastry is as fun to say as it is to eat.

Sugar syrup:
1 ¼ cups sugar
¾ cup water
⅓ cup honey
1 4-inch strip zest from lemon
1 tablespoon lemon juice
½ teaspoon cinnamon
⅛ teaspoon ground cloves
⅛ teaspoon salt

Nut filling:
8 ounces walnuts
4 ounces pistachios
1 ¼ teaspoons cinnamon
¼ teaspoon ground cloves
2 tablespoons sugar
⅛ teaspoon salt

Pastry and butter:
3 sticks butter, melted
1 pound phyllo dough, thawed according to package directions

For syrup: Bring ingredients to a boil in a saucepan, set aside to cool. Remove zest.

For filling: Chop nuts finely. Combine with remaining ingredients.

To assemble: Brush 13x9-inch pan with butter. Place 8 phyllo sheets in bottom, brushing each with butter before adding next. Spread one-third of filling over sheets. Repeat twice with 6 more sheets and the remaining filling. Finish with 8 to 10 sheets. Press down sheets. Spoon 4 tablespoons butter over top.

Using a serrated knife, cut baklava into diamond-shaped pieces. Bake at 300 degrees about 1½ hours or until golden and crisp, rotating pan once. After removing from oven, pour syrup over the lines cut into the baklava. Let cool before serving.

Spanakopita (Spinach Pie)
Source: Tonya Jett and Eva Pappas

3 packages (10 ounces each) frozen chopped spinach, thawed
2 medium onions, chopped
¼ cup olive oil or butter
¼ cup minced parsley
¼ cup lemon juice
Salt and pepper, to taste
4 eggs
1 cup cottage cheese
1½ cups feta cheese
1 pound phyllo dough, thawed according to package directions
3 sticks butter, melted or clarified

Drain spinach thoroughly in colander, squeezing out excess moisture.

In a large skillet, sauté onions in olive oil or butter. Add spinach, parsley, lemon juice and seasonings. Cook until liquid evaporates.

In a large bowl, combine eggs and cheese. Stir in spinach mixture, blending well. Set aside.

Take phyllo dough out of plastic bag and carefully unfold. Butter a 13x9-inch pan.

Working with 1 phyllo sheet at a time, lay each sheet in the pan and generously spread with melted butter. Repeat for 10 sheets, trimming the edges to fit the pan.

Spread spinach-cheese mixture evenly over phyllo. Top with remaining phyllo, buttering each sheet and trimming the edges.

Let sit in refrigerator for 30 minutes. Remove and score in squares with sharp knife. Bake at 325 degrees for 1½ hours or until golden brown.

Note: Filling should not be juicy or bottom layers of phyllo will be soggy.

Ghoraibi (Lebanese Shortbread Cookie)
Source: Sherry Abraham

2 sticks butter
1½ cups sugar
3 cups flour

Cream butter until it is light and fluffy. Gradually add sugar, a little at a time, mixing well as you are adding it. After adding the sugar, mix for an additional 2 to 3 minutes. Gradually mix in flour.

Refrigerate for 30 minutes.

Place oven rack in center of oven. Heat oven to 325 degrees.

Take a small amount of mixture and shape it into a ball about 1 inch in diameter. Using the palms of your hands, roll into a 3-inch finger-shaped roll. Place on an ungreased cookie sheet and twist into an S shape. Score the top slightly with a fork.

Bake for 15 minutes. The cookies will remain white after baked. Let cookies cool at least 2 hours before removing. Store covered at room temperature.

*Hummus
The ingredients for just about every hummus recipe are the same, but different cooks use different proportions. Adjust them until you find the version you like.
Source: Gigi Shadid

2 cans (15 ounces) chickpeas, drained
¾ cup freshly squeezed lemon juice
¾ cup tahini (sesame paste)

Salt, to taste
2 cloves garlic
Garnish: Olive oil, paprika and parsley

Drain water from chickpeas. Put all ingredients except the garnish in food processor or blender with ¼ cup water. Process until smooth. Drizzle with olive oil and sprinkle with paprika and parsley, if desired. Serve with pita triangles.

Stuffed Grape Leaves

Some of the cooks who prepare these delicious bites for St. Mary's annual dinner and bake sale cultivate their own grape plants for the leaves. As one cook told me, your stuffed grape leaves will improve with practice.

Source: Alberta Busada

1 jar (8 ounces) grape leaves
1½ pounds lean ground beef
2 cups uncooked rice
1 can (15 ounces) diced or crushed tomatoes, with juices
5½ teaspoons salt, divided use
2 teaspoons cinnamon
¾ teaspoon pepper
1 teaspoon garlic powder
4 cups water
⅓ cup lemon juice

Remove grape leaves from bottle, discarding juice, and separate.

In a bowl, combine beef, rice, tomatoes, 2½ teaspoons salt, cinnamon, pepper and garlic powder.

Lay a grape leaf flat so that its veined side faces up and its smooth side is down (remove stem if present). Place about 1 tablespoon of the meat mixture in the center of the leaf. Fold the bottom of the grape leaf over the mixture; fold in the sides, then continue rolling up the grape leaf. Repeat with remaining grape leaves and filling.

Place grape leaves in a large pot. Combine water, 3 teaspoons salt and lemon juice in a bowl and stir until salt is dissolved. Pour over stuffed grape leaves. If necessary, add water until leaves are covered. Bring to a boil, reduce heat and simmer about 30 minutes, or until leaves and rice are tender. Pour off excess water, then carefully remove stuffed grape leaves from pot using tongs.

Chicken with Rice and Chickpeas

Toni Shadid was a well-known restaurateur and caterer who cooked pre-game meals for the Wichita State men's basketball team. This recipe is one she made for family meals.
Source: Toni Shadid

2 pounds bone-in chicken breasts
Water
2 cups uncooked long-grain rice
¼ cup clarified butter, olive oil or regular butter
1 large onion, sliced
2 cans (16 ounces each) chickpeas, drained and rinsed
2 teaspoons salt
1 teaspoon pepper
1 teaspoon cinnamon

Place chicken breasts in a Dutch oven or large saucepot and add enough water to just cover. Bring to a boil, then cover and reduce heat to simmer.

Cook about 30 minutes or until chicken is done. Let chicken stand in cooking liquid until cool enough to handle, then remove chicken to a cutting board. Discard the skin and shred meat. Skim off any impurities from the broth and pour it in a bowl.

Meanwhile, place rice in a microwave-safe container. Cover rice with water and microwave for 7 minutes on high. Carefully remove container from microwave and drain off water.

In the Dutch oven or pot, melt the butter and sauté the onion until soft. Add

Famed for her energy, the late Toni Shadid didn't even have time to brush off her apron before posing for this photo with her husband, Danny, in front of their restaurant and catering business.

the chickpeas and seasonings. Layer the chicken on top of the chickpeas and the rice on top of the chicken.

Pour about 4 cups of the reserved broth over the rice, or enough to come just below the top of the rice.

Bring liquid to a boil, then cover pot and reduce heat to a simmer. Cook about 20 minutes, then turn off heat and let pot stand about 30 minutes.

When ready to serve, carefully turn mixture in pot onto a large platter to produce layers of rice, chicken and chickpeas.

Chapter 4

EL PUEBLO, MI PUEBLO

In Wichita, there's a place where Spanish is spoken as frequently as English, where food carts peddle freshly made churros and elote, and Norteno music blasts from pickup trucks getting loving attention at the self-operated carwash. Where you can find food trucks cranking out tacos and tortas and burritos into the wee hours of the morning, to be enjoyed on plastic tables set up in parking lots.

Doesn't sound familiar? Then you haven't been to the north-side neighborhood known as "El Pueblo" (often referred to as "The Barrio").

And your stomach is *furioso* at you!

Before regaling you with tales of melt-in-your-mouth carnitas, citrusy ceviche and steaming bowls of pozole you've been missing, a little history. Mexican immigrants and their descendants have been in Wichita since its earliest days, when it was the terminus of cattle drives up the Chisholm Trail from Texas. One 1872 newspaper article referred to "Mexicans and Texans" throwing away their hard-earned money in the city's gambling halls.

The coming of railroads brought some Mexicans as permanent residents, and the opening of nearby meatpacking plants attracted more, although their numbers remained small. The 1915 census listed 135 Mexicans living here. According to a history of the area compiled by Wichita State University, the railroads offered Mexican immigrants housing to lure them here. That turned out to be mainly old boxcars and shacks located along the tracks.

By the 1920s, according to the WSU history, there were ten small Hispanic enclaves along railroad tracks between Lincoln in the south ("South Yard"),

Tacos served with tall glasses of Horchata (made from rice) and Agua de Jamaica (made from hibiscus flowers) are staples of Mexican restaurants in Wichita.

24th Street in the north ("El Rock Island"), St. Francis in the west ("El Barrio de la Cuatro") and Wabash in the east. The population grew and gradually became concentrated north and south of 21st Street, between Broadway and Waco. As it did, 21st Street developed into a business district for more than just the local Hispanic population. The Nomar Theater opened at Market and 21st in 1929 with a segregated balcony for Mexican and Black customers and seating for whites below.

CHURCH AND CHILES

Our Lady of Perpetual Help Catholic Church has been a key part of the neighborhood since its founding in 1927, and that's where my education in authentic Mexican cooking began. On an assignment for the *Eagle*, I watched as female parishioners prepared food for the church's annual series of Lenten dinners, realizing that much of what I thought I knew about Mexican food was wrong. Although similar to the Tex-Mex dishes many of us grew up on, the emphasis was on corn tortillas versus flour ones and chile-based sauces versus tomato-laden salsas (although flour tortillas and tomatoes had their place, of course). Everything was not smothered in melted cheese (although cheese was used, and in more varieties than I realized). Oh, and there were no chips, not at the church's dinner or at any of the neighborhood's restaurants I began frequenting. That's not to say Mexican Americans don't eat chips; they do, usually with freshly made guacamole. They just don't start off every meal with a huge basket of them and a saucer of salsa. That's a Tex-Mex thing.

Much of the work to produce this food was painstaking: for instance, toasting dried chile pods, then rehydrating and pulverizing them to make fresh enchilada sauce. Tortillas were softened in hot oil before being filled for those enchiladas. Taking the place of salsa was chunky pico de gallo, made by finely chopping fresh tomatoes, onion, chiles and cilantro. In these church ladies' hands, the food was fresh, festive and a bit fiery thanks to liberal use of fresh and dried chiles.

A mural on the side of a tortilleria in north Wichita colorfully depicts ancient cooking methods still used today in local homes and restaurants.

As I was to discover, this was just one style of Mexican cooking, though at that time probably the one most prevalent in Wichita. The city's longest-running Mexican restaurant, Connie's on North Broadway, was started in 1967 by Concepcion Lopez, who'd made her name cooking for the church dinners. Felipe's, La Chinita and Chico's have also fed Wichitans for decades.

TACO TOWN

In more recent years, the cooking of many regions of Mexico has made its way here, from Tijuana and Monterrey to Guadalajara and the Yucatan.

I live in North Riverside, which lies just south of El Pueblo. Through the years, I've been in nearly every restaurant, grocery, bakery, tortilleria and fruit stand that's operated there. On weekend mornings, restaurants that specialize in seafood and are known as *mariscos* are the place to get huge goblets of shrimp in a spicy cocktail sauce. On summer nights, it's time to get in line for one of dozens of flavors of ice cream made by Palateria La Reyna on North Arkansas (or wait for one of its bicycle-powered ice cream

Small taquerias like this one open on a regular basis in Wichita, often serving amazing food before quickly going out of business. Fortunately, this one relocated to a bigger space on North Broadway.

Molino's owners Mario and Mara Quiroz specialize in grilled tacos called piratas and other food of their native Monterrey, Mexico.

wagons to cruise by). If you're cooking at home, you can score fifty steaming-hot corn tortillas wrapped in white paper for $2.50 at Tortilleria Rodriguez on Waco.

Today, Hispanics officially constitute about 10 percent of the city's population and authentic Mexican food is no longer limited to El Pueblo. Restaurateurs such as Mario and Mara Quiroz, the owners of Molino's Taqueria, have succeeded with locations elsewhere, while entrepreneurs such as Eddie Sandoval of Pinole Blue, which makes blue corn tortillas, are important parts of the city's younger foodie crowd. It would be surprising if there aren't at least one hundred Mexican restaurants in operation. El Rio Bravo, a huge Mexican market that opened in the south part of Wichita, proved so popular with its inexpensive produce and tennis court–length meat counter that a second one opened on the north side. In other words, there's deliciously authentic Mexican food available across the city.

But for me, there's still nothing like a late-night taco eaten in El Pueblo.

*Enchiladas

These vegetarian enchiladas are prepared for Lenten dinners at Our Lady of Perpetual Help Church. They're also delicious filled with cooked meat, seafood, beans and other vegetables. The enchiladas can be eaten immediately or are a great make-ahead dish.
Source: Elena Gonzalez and Felicitas Urbina

Oil for frying
Corn or flour tortillas

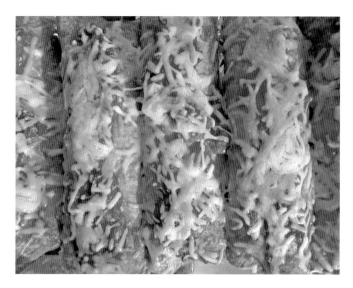

Enchilada means "to add chile pepper to" in Spanish. Enchiladas are traditionally made by coating flour or corn tortillas with a chile-based sauce, then rolling them around a variety of fillings.

Enchilada sauce, store-bought or homemade (see following recipe)
2 pounds potatoes, boiled, peeled and mashed
1 can (16 ounces) peas, drained and added to potatoes
1 bag (12 ounces) shredded cheddar cheese
3 tablespoons chopped onions, added to cheese
Pico de gallo (see recipe below)

Heat a tablespoon of oil in skillet over medium heat. One at a time, fry tortillas about 10 seconds on each side, turning with tongs, then dredge both sides in enchilada sauce before placing on large tray. Repeat with remaining tortillas.

To assemble an enchilada, spoon about ¼ to ⅓ cup potato-pea mixture onto one-half of a tortilla and top with 1 to 2 tablespoons cheese-onion mixture. Roll the tortilla up and place on serving tray. Top with additional cheese and serve with pico de gallo.

Notes: If making ahead, place enchiladas in a baking pan covered with aluminum foil and refrigerate. When ready, cook at 350 degrees about 20 to 30 minutes or until heated through. For a lighter version of the dish, soften tortillas by microwaving about 20 seconds instead of frying in oil.

Enchilada Sauce

The dried chiles used in this recipe can be found in Mexican markets and in the Mexican aisles of many supermarkets. In deciding which chile pod to use, the general rule of thumb is the smaller the chile, the hotter it is.
Source: Elena Gonzalez and Felicitas Urbina

4 dried chile anchos
8 dried chile pods
Water
1 garlic clove, peeled
½ teaspoon ground cumin
½ teaspoon salt

In pot, cover chile anchos and chile pods with water and cook on a light boil until rehydrated and tender, about 10 minutes. Remove from water and cool. With knife, split open chiles and rinse away seeds under running water. Place chile anchos and chile pods in blender, along with garlic, cumin and salt. Add water about three-quarters of the way up chiles. Puree until sauce is smooth.

*Pico de Gallo

Guacamole and two types of salsa await diners at one of Wichita's many Mexican restaurants.

Pico de gallo is simply fresh, chunky salsa—about the best use of fresh Kansas tomatoes I can think of. The amounts called for in the recipe are a starting point; taste and adjust as you see fit. Bell pepper, cucumber and minced garlic are sometimes added. Using tomatoes of different colors will give the pico de gallo an especially attractive appearance.

3–5 ripe tomatoes
1 white or yellow onion
1–2 jalapeño(s), seeds removed
1 bunch cilantro
Juice of 1 lime
Salt and pepper, to taste

Chop and combine all ingredients. Cover and let flavors meld at least 30 minutes before serving.

Grilled Steak Piratas

It didn't long for word to get out about Frida's when it opened on West
21st Street in 2008. Owners Mara and Mario Quiroz served piratas and
charro beans from their native state of Monterrey, Mexico. That first
location proved inadequate, and today the couple operate two locations
of Molino's Taqueria.

Source: Mara and Mario Quiroz

Marinade:
1 cup orange juice
1 teaspoon lime juice
1 teaspoon seasoned salt, preferably Lawry's
1 teaspoon salt
1 teaspoon pepper
1 teaspoon garlic powder, or 2 cloves garlic, minced

2–3 pounds flap steak or thinly sliced sirloin

For piratas:
Flour tortillas
Shredded Mexican cheese
Chopped lettuce
Pico de gallo
Guacamole
Sour cream

Combine marinade ingredients in a bowl or sealable plastic bag. Place
2 to 3 pounds flap steak or thinly sliced sirloin steak in the marinade
for 1 to 2 hours.

Remove meat from marinade; grill until desired doneness is
reached. To make piratas, fill tortillas with steak, cheese, lettuce, pico
de gallo, guacamole and sour cream. Heat in skillet or sandwich press
until toasty.

Charro Beans

Anybody who thinks beans are boring has not tried the ones served at Molino's, which are liberally spiked with jalapeño, garlic, bacon, hot dogs and, yes, pork rinds.
Source: Mara and Mario Quiroz

1 pound dry pinto beans
Water
Chicken broth, if needed
1 jalapeño, seeded and chopped
4 cloves garlic, minced
5 slices bacon, cooked and chopped
4 hot dogs, cooked and chopped
2 cups pork rinds
Salt and pepper

To make the beans: Soak beans and cook according to package directions. Beans should be a little soupy when cooked. If not, add 1 to 2 cups chicken broth.

Add jalapeño, garlic, bacon, hot dogs and pork rinds and continue cooking about 30 minutes. Season to taste with salt and pepper.

*Chilaquiles

This dish is a smart way to use up leftovers. For a breakfast version, omit the chicken, scrambling a couple of eggs with the crisp tortilla strips.
Source: Mara and Mario Quiroz

Corn tortillas
Oil, for frying
Mild red or green salsa
Cooked and shredded chicken
Shredded Monterey Jack cheese
Fried eggs (optional)

Cut tortillas into strips. In a large frying pan, heat oil, then add strips and cook, stirring, until golden brown and crisp. Add salsa to pan, then chicken and cheese, stirring all together. Turn onto plate and serve. If desired, top with fried egg(s).

Timbale

Celia Gorlich's recipe for this unusual dish has a fun backstory: her grandmother used it to win a suitor's hand in Mexico City. A timbale is a stacked enchilada that's *really* stacked—12 tortillas piled on top of each other, each separated by a layer of chorizo-egg filling, the whole thing smothered in tomato sauce and cheese and then baked. The recipe makes 8 generous servings.

3 packages (10 ounces each) chorizo
12 eggs, lightly beaten
1 can (28 ounces) tomato sauce
1½ tablespoons Mexican seasoning (or your own combination of chile powder, cumin, red pepper and salt)
1 clove garlic, minced
Vegetable oil, for frying tortillas
1 pound shredded cheddar-jack cheese
2 medium yellow onions, chopped
12 corn tortillas (6- or 8-inch round)

Remove chorizo from package and cook over medium heat in large skillet, breaking up, about 5 minutes or until fat is rendered out. Cool slightly, then carefully pour off grease. Pat chorizo in pan with paper towels to remove remaining grease.

Push chorizo to one side of skillet and add lightly beaten eggs to skillet. Cook until eggs begin to set, stirring into chorizo to combine. Turn off heat.

Empty tomato sauce into a saucepan, add Mexican seasoning and garlic and cook, stirring, until heated through. Turn off heat.

In another saucepan or skillet, heat about 1 inch vegetable oil over medium-high heat.

Place shredded cheese and chopped onion in two separate bowls.

To assemble the timbale, use tongs to submerge a tortilla in the hot oil for 10 seconds, or until it softens. Lift the tortilla out of the oil and place it in the tomato sauce. Use a spoon to turn it until both sides are lightly coated with tomato sauce.

With the spoon, lay the coated tortilla flat in a baking dish or on a baking sheet. Use another spoon to spread ½ cup of the chorizo-egg mixture over the tortilla; sprinkle with ¼ cup chopped onion and ¼ cup shredded cheese.

Repeat with remaining tortillas and ingredients until you have 12 layers of tortillas. Press the layers down as you go to help stabilize the timbale. (You may have some ingredients left over.)

Pour remaining tomato sauce over the top layer of chorizo, onion and cheese, then top with another ½ cup of shredded cheese.

Place the timbale in a preheated 350-degree oven and cook 20 minutes. Remove from oven and let sit about 5 minutes before slicing, cake-style.

Serve with accompanying recipes for timbale salsa and guacamole.

Timbale Salsa

Celia Gorlich says this salsa is best made one day in advance. Its tartness cuts the richness of the timbale.

1 yellow onion, chopped
1 can (16 ounces) diced tomatoes, drained
1 ½ tablespoons dried oregano
White vinegar

Put onion, tomatoes and oregano in a small bowl. Add enough vinegar to come up to top of mixture.

Guacamole

2 ripe avocados, peeled and seed removed
2 tablespoons extra-virgin olive oil
¼ teaspoon garlic salt, or to taste
2 tablespoons salsa (optional)

Mash avocados. Add remaining ingredients.

*Ceviche

El Paisa on north Arkansas may never have been more successful than when it operated as a tiny, twenty-four-hour take-out joint. Its later incarnation as a sit-down restaurant brought about several changes in ownership, closures and reopenings. Through it all, however, dishes like this kept customers coming back.

Source: El Paisa

6 tilapia fillets (about 1¼ pounds)
8 limes
1 teaspoon salt
1 teaspoon black pepper
1 cup cilantro, freshly chopped
1 cup yellow onion, diced
1 cup fresh tomato, chopped
1 jalapeño pepper, diced, or hot sauce to taste
1 cup bottled clam juice
1 ripe avocado, peeled and sliced

Cut the tilapia fillets into ¼-inch cubes and place in a mixing bowl. Squeeze the juice of 8 limes over the fish and toss lightly. Add salt and pepper. Cover and refrigerate for 4 hours (the acid in the lime juice will "cook" the fish, making it firm and white).

Pour off the lime juice. Stir in the cilantro, onion, tomato, jalapeño and clam juice. Mound mixture on plate and top with avocado slices.

Serve cold with tostadas or corn chips.

*Mexican Street Corn

This recipe and the one that follows for Mexican Fruit Salad are served at stands along West 21st Street and North Broadway. As with pico de gallo, proportions are a matter of individual taste. Mexican crema and cojita cheese are available in Hispanic markets and many supermarkets.

Mayonnaise and/or Mexican crema (or regular sour cream)
Shredded cotija cheese (parmesan can be substituted)
Chile powder
Chopped cilantro
Salt and pepper
Fresh ears of corn, husks removed
Limes, quartered

In a bowl, combine mayonnaise and/or crema, cheese, chile powder, cilantro, salt and pepper to taste. Grill corn over medium high heat about 4 to 5 minutes per side, or until kernels are tender and starting to char (corn can be boiled or cooked in microwave if no grill is available). Brush mayonnaise mixture over corn and serve with lime quarters.

*Mexican Fruit Salad

Serving sweet fruit with spicy and sour ingredients seems counterintuitive, but the contrast creates an amazing burst of flavor. Look for the Tajin brand chile powder and Chamoy brand hot sauce, available in Hispanic markets and some supermarkets. Tamarind straws, which are straws coated with a sweet-sour candy, are often added as a final flourish when the fruit salad is served in cups.

Melon (such as watermelon, cantaloupe and honeydew)
Fresh pineapple
Mango and/or papaya (optional)
Jicama and/or cucumber (optional)
Fresh lime juice
Chile powder
Mexican hot sauce
Salt and pepper

Peel rind and skin from melon, fruit and vegetables (if using), discarding seeds where present. Cut into bite-size chunks. Place in serving bowl or individual cups and garnish to taste with lime juice, chile powder, hot sauce, salt and pepper.

Coctel de Camarones (Shrimp Cocktail)

You can enjoy versions of this in several *mariscos* along North Broadway.

Onion, chopped
Celery, chopped
Fresh lime juice
Cilantro

Fresh tomatoes
Ketchup
Clamato (a mixture of tomato and clam juice)
Jalapeño, seeded and minced
Cucumber, peeled, seeded and chopped
Jicama, peeled and chopped
Hot pepper sauce
Large cooked shrimp
Salt and pepper, to taste
Ripe avocado, cut into chunks
Saltines and tortilla chips, for serving

Combine all ingredients except for avocados, saltines and chips in a large bowl. Refrigerate 1 hour. Just before serving, add avocado. Divide between ice cream sundae glasses or large beer schooners and serve with saltines and chips.

Molcajete

Within days of tasting this dish at El Torero in Wichita, I went back to ask for the recipe. That restaurant and a second location in Derby are both now gone. Molcajete is traditionally served in the heated stone bowl—the Mexican version of a mortar and pestle—from which it takes its name. This recipe calls for a serving dish that can be placed in the oven and heated.
Source: El Torero

Tomatillo salsa:
1½ chile de arbos (dried chiles)
2 cans (11 ounces each) tomatillos, liquid reserved
¼ cup onion, chopped
¼ bunch cilantro, chopped
1 large clove garlic, chopped

Vegetable oil
8 ounces chicken breast, sliced as for fajitas
16 shrimp, peeled
Salt

1 cup each onion and tomato, chopped
1 cup tomatillo salsa (store-bought or from recipe above)

Garnish:
4 green onions
½ avocado, cut into fourths
2 tomatoes, sliced
¼ cup onion, chopped
¼ cup cilantro, chopped
1 cup shredded cheese

Place oven-safe serving dish in 250-degree oven. Make tomatillo salsa by following recipe below. Heat to simmering and pour 1 cup into serving dish; return serving dish to oven.

Heat vegetable oil in skillet set over medium heat. Sauté chicken and shrimp until done; season to taste with salt. Remove mixture from skillet and add to serving dish in oven.

Add a bit of vegetable oil to skillet and quickly sauté 1 cup onion and 1 cup tomato until onion is soft. Add to serving dish.

Lay green onions, avocado slices and tomato slices on top of meat and vegetables. Top with chopped onion, cilantro and cheese. Serve with warm tortillas.

To make tomatillo salsa: Toast chile de arbos in skillet until fragrant. Combine with other ingredients in a blender or food processor; process until well blended.

*Carnitas
Wichita Eagle restaurant writer Denise Neil doesn't just write about food. She's an eminently entertaining dinner party host whose specialty—carnitas—would do any authentic Mexican restaurant proud. I've extensively consulted her restaurant coverage for the *Eagle* while putting together this book.
Source: Denise Neil

2 teaspoons ground cumin
1 teaspoon ground coriander seed
2 teaspoons kosher salt

2 teaspoons chile powder (ancho or New Mexico recommended, but regular works)
3 pounds boneless Boston butt, cut into 1½- to 2-inch pieces, excess fat trimmed
¼ cup olive oil
½ cup red wine vinegar
1 tablespoon honey
½ cup chicken stock or canned chicken broth
1 large onion, diced

Mix cumin, coriander, salt and chile power together. Add pork to the mixture and toss well to coat. Cover the bowl and put in the refrigerator for several hours or overnight.

In a large covered pot, heat the olive oil over medium-high heat. Cook the pork in batches until browned on all sides, about 10 minutes. Transfer pork to a plate as it's cooked. When it's all browned, set the pot aside. Do not drain.

In a small bowl, stir the vinegar with the honey until the honey dissolves. Stir in the chicken stock and add the mixture to the pot, scraping up any browned bits on the bottom. Add the onion and bring the liquid to a boil over high heat. Lower the heat to maintain a simmer, return the pork to the pot cover and cook, stirring occasionally, until the pork is fork-tender, at least 2 hours.

Remove the cover and increase the heat slightly. Continue to cook until the liquid has evaporated and the fat from the pork is bubbling, about 30 minutes. As soon as the pork begins to brown, stir regularly to prevent burning. It's done when it has become golden to dark brown and is nicely crisped. Shred by hand. Serve on its own or as a filling for tacos, burritos, etc.

Chile Rellenos

This recipe from Chico's is certainly labor-intensive, but the payoff comes when you bite into one of the rellenos, tasting in succession Ranchero sauce, golden brown coating, roasted pepper and savory beef-cheese-potato filling. The coating is made by whipping egg whites to soft peaks, then adding back in the egg yolks. For best results, serve as soon after frying as possible.
Source: Jose Arnoldo Fernandez

10 Anaheim chiles
1 pound ground beef
½ onion, chopped
1 teaspoon salt
½ teaspoon pepper
½ teaspoon garlic powder
1 teaspoon cumin
½ potato, cooked, peeled and diced
2 cups shredded American cheese
Flour, for dusting chiles
10 eggs, separated
Oil for frying

Ranchero sauce:
2 cups bell pepper, chopped
2 cups onion, chopped
2 cups tomato, chopped
Salt, pepper and garlic powder, to taste
Juice from canned or bottled jalapeños
Hot sauce

Prepare chiles by first roasting them. There are several ways to do this. Chico's method is to deep-fry the chiles about 3 minutes, then cool and peel off the thin transparent skin. Whichever method you use, do not cook the chiles until they are too fragile to hold the filling. When the skin is removed, slit open the chiles on one side and remove the seeds. Leave the stem on.

For the filling, brown the hamburger with the onion, then add salt and pepper, garlic powder and cumin. Stir in the diced potato.

Divide the hamburger mixture and the cheese among the chiles; close the chile opening with toothpicks. Dust the stuffed chiles with flour.

Separate the whites and yolks of the eggs into two bowls. Whip the egg whites with an electric beater until peaks form, then beat in the egg yolks with a pinch of flour until just incorporated.

Heat about 1 inch of oil in a heavy skillet. When the oil is hot, hold a chile by the stem and dip into the beaten eggs until well coated. Lay the chile in the skillet; it will puff up immediately. When the bottom is golden brown, turn the chile over with tongs and cook until it is the same color. Remove from oil, set on paper towels to drain and keep warm while frying remaining chiles.

Serve chile rellenos with Ranchero sauce.

To make Ranchero sauce, heat vegetable oil in skillet and sauté bell pepper, onion and tomato until vegetables are soft and release their moisture. Season to taste with salt, pepper, garlic powder, jalapeño juice and hot sauce. Sauce should be the consistency of medium chunky salsa. If too dry, add water. If too thin, make a slurry of equal parts flour and water and add, 1 teaspoon at a time, to sauce while cooking.

Food Truck Grilled Chicken

The grilled chicken at El Pollo Dorado, prepared on an outdoor grill, sends a tantalizing aroma up and down West 21st Street. *Photo by Carrie Rengers.*

Originally a food truck parked at 21st Street and Wellington, El Pollo Dorado now operates as a big outdoor grill surrounded by piles of wood imported from Mexico. The cook told me the ingredients in the marinade used to make its fantastic chicken. He didn't divulge the exact quantities, but these work well. Get a whiff of the place and I can almost guarantee you'll stop.

Source: El Pollo Dorado

Marinade:

1 cup pineapple juice
¼ cup orange juice
2 tablespoons olive oil
6 cloves garlic, minced
1 package (1.41 ounces) Sazon seasoning, available in Hispanic aisle of supermarket
2 teaspoons salt

1 chicken, about 5 pounds, cut into six or eight pieces

Combine the marinade ingredients in a large bowl or plastic sealable bag. Stir or shake ingredients until Sazon seasoning dissolves. Add chicken pieces and let marinate 1 hour. Remove chicken from marinade and grill about 1 hour or until juices run clear when pierced with a fork (about 160 to 165 degrees internal temperature).

Gorditas

Dona Lupe thrived for a while in a small strip center on north Amidon, thanks in part to owner Guadalupe Villarreal's supple way with the savory stuffed pastries known as gorditas.
Makes about 20 gorditas.
Source: Guadalupe Villarreal

4 cups instant masa mix (a corn flour available in Hispanic markets
and some supermarkets)
3¼ cups water
I can refried beans, heated
I cup shredded Mexican cheese
Optional garnishes: Salsa, hot sauce, shredded lettuce, chopped onion

Place masa mix in bowl and add water; knead with your hands for several minutes. The dough should be moist but not stick to your hands.

Keeping your hands damp, break off a piece of dough (about ⅓ cup) and roll it into a ball. Flatten the ball slightly and then place between two sheets of wax paper; press down with the bottom of a plate until the gordita is about 5 inches across and about ¼ inch thick.

Peel the gordita off the wax paper and use your finger to smooth any cracks along the edge of the tortilla. The edge must be sealed so that steam can collect inside the gordita.

Place the gordita on an ungreased cast-iron or nonstick skillet set over medium heat. Cook, turning occasionally, until brown spots appear on the gordita and it puffs slightly, about 8 minutes. Repeat with remaining dough.

When the gorditas are done, cut a pocket along one side as you would with pita bread and fill with refried beans, cheese and garnishes, if desired. The gorditas can be made up to a day ahead of time and stored in a resealable bag, then filled and reheated.

Note: Making gorditas is an art that takes some practice. If you can't get your gorditas to puff up from trapped steam as the accompanying recipe calls for, try frying them in oil instead and then top with beans and cheese to make sopas.

Carne Asada Torta

Tortas are the Mexican version of a sandwich, and yes, all these things typically go on one. In fact, this version from Nunez Mexican Grill on Harry Street is not even the most extravagant I've seen (or eaten).
Source: Caterino Nunez

Bolillo (a crusty baguette-like bread available in Mexican bakeries
and some supermarkets)
Refried beans
Guacamole
Mayonnaise
Carne asada (see recipe below; other cooked meat can be substituted)
Shredded lettuce
Tomato slices
Chopped onion
Chopped cilantro
Shredded mozzarella cheese
Green or red salsa
Chopped jalapeños (optional)

Slice bolillo in half lengthwise. Butter and toast inside surfaces in a pan. Spread a thin layer of refried beans on bottom layer. Stir together guacamole and mayonnaise (4 parts guacamole to 1 part mayo) and spread over beans. Top with remaining ingredients and serve.

Carne Asada

Although carne asada is usually made with beef, this recipe calls for pork.
Source: Caterino Nunez

Marinade:
1 ounce achiote powder, optional (available in Hispanic groceries
and some supermarkets)
1 cup pineapple juice
1 cup vinegar
3 tablespoons minced garlic

½ cup salsa verde
½ teaspoon salt
½ teaspoon pepper

2–3 pounds pork loin roast, sliced into ¼-inch-thick pieces

Combine marinade ingredients. Add pork slices, turn to coat evenly and refrigerate at least 2 hours.

When ready to cook, sauté in a lightly oiled pan over medium heat until done.

Christmas Tamales

Sweet tamales are a Christmas tradition in Wichita, and not just among Hispanic families. Hispanic grocers report that many Anglos have gotten into the habit of buying masa, the refrigerated mixture of ground corn, water and lard that's the starting point for sweet and savory tamales. Dry instant mixes are available in Hispanic markets and some supermarkets, but some cooks feel they are not as good. Corn husks are also found in some supermarkets.
Source: Thala Ramirez

1 package corn husks
5 pounds prepared masa (available at Hispanic groceries)
2 cups raisins
1 cup coconut, flaked
2 cups crushed pineapple, drained
3 cups sugar
1 cup piloncillo (available in Hispanic markets) or 1 cup brown sugar plus 2 teaspoons cinnamon
1 tablespoon baking powder

Separate corn husks into four or five bundles and place in a large container of warm water for 30 minutes. While the husks soak, mix remaining ingredients together with your hands. Wring out a bundle of husks.

Spread about ¼ cup of the sweetened masa mixture in the middle of a corn husk's smooth side, making a square or rectangular shape.

Fold the husk in from the sides and then over from the pointy end. If desired, tie with a thin strip of husk. Repeat with remaining husks and masa mixture.

Place tamales open side up in steamer or traditional tamale cooker with water, bring to a boil and cook covered about 1 hour, or until husk easily separates from tamale. Let sit about 5 minutes before serving. Tamales can be reheated in a microwave.

Chapter 5

FRIEND OF PHO

Like a first kiss, a novice's first bowl of pho can be an intoxicating, mysterious thing. I still remember mine, eaten in the old Pho 99 restaurant on North Broadway more than twenty years ago. It arrived in a huge bowl, with the steam rising from the broth making it difficult to identify contents below the surface. What were those thin slices of meat? Okay, beef. But why were some pieces raw? Oh, now I see, they're being cooked by the heat of the broth. Hmm, here's a meatball and there's a strip of chewy tendon. Maneuver chopsticks to get at the huge pile of rice noodles tucked under the meat. Then back to the spoon to scoop up more of the fabulously fragrant broth, exotic and comforting at the same time. I could hardly blow on it fast enough to get it into my mouth.

I fell hard for pho and Vietnamese cuisine in general.

Today, I like to brag that for a city its size, Wichita boasts the best Vietnamese food in the country. I can't prove this, of course. Just call it a gut feeling, from someone's who put *a lot* of Vietnamese food in his gut.

By conservative estimate, I've eaten at least one hundred bowls of pho in Wichita. I've come away disappointed only once. That doesn't count all the banh mi sandwiches, spring rolls, crawfish, stir fries, café sua and other Vietnamese specialties consumed with a similar success rate.

I'm hardly the only American-born resident who feels this way. Walk into any of the city's Vietnamese restaurants and non-Vietnamese customers usually predominate, not only "foodies" but downtown businesspeople, airmen from McConnell Air Force Base, college students, construction

Right: Wichitans love debating which Vietnamese restaurant serves the best bowl of pho. Whichever place you choose, the best advice is to come hungry.

Opposite: Shopping in one of the city's Asian markets is like taking a quick trip to the other side of the world.

workers and cops. They post photos on Facebook and argue over which place is best. Twenty Vietnamese restaurants were operating here in early 2021, far more than needed to serve residents of Vietnamese backgrounds.

By comparison, a friend once took me to what was purported to be the best Vietnamese restaurant in Chicago. Its pho would have ranked just slightly above the single mediocre bowl I mentioned eating here.

WAVES OF REFUGEES

The first wave of Vietnamese immigrants arrived in Wichita after the fall of the South Vietnam government in 1975. Most of these 1,500 or so newcomers were former military and government officials and their families who left with the Americans and spent a short time at the refugee camp in Fort Chaffee, Arkansas. Many were sponsored in their move to Wichita by the Catholic and Lutheran churches.

The second influx of refugees, about twice as large, arrived in the late 1970s and early 1980s after fleeing their native country's Communist regime. Some were "boat people" and others walked out of Vietnam, but nearly all survived challenging if not harrowing experiences before reaching the United States. Jimmy Nguyen was one of them. Rather than be forced into military service, he paid a guide to lead him out of Vietnam, through Cambodia and to a refugee camp in Thailand in 1981. "I saw a lot of dead

people along the way," he told me for a story in the *Eagle*. After initially settling in Houston, Nguyen moved to Wichita and opened Thai Binh, the city's largest Asian market, in 1984.

Hanh Bui, owner of the city's oldest Vietnamese restaurant, also was part of the second wave. He and his wife, Hai, fled Vietnam by boat and came here in 1981 after spending time as refugees in Hong Kong. Bui moved to Dodge City for a job in a meatpacking plant, returned in 1989 and went to work as a waiter at Saigon Oriental Restaurant. He bought the restaurant in 1990.

Continued immigration combined with births of children and grandchildren have brought the city's population with a Vietnamese background to about ten thousand. That's 2.4 percent of the city's total, which is about five times bigger than the national average. But I don't think it's just the size of that community that accounts for the surplus of great Vietnamese food; I think it's due to the presence of a wider, receptive audience.

PHO FEVER SPREADS

Early customers of the city's Vietnamese restaurants included ex–American servicemen who'd gotten hooked on the food while serving in southeast Asia. Vietnamese home cooks, meanwhile, shared their food with Wichitans who were helping them adjust to life here. The Vietnamese are justifiably proud of their cuisine. I haven't met one yet who isn't happy to explain an ingredient or technique, insisting you take home some of whatever they are preparing. Vietnamese cooking has been called one of the most beautiful cuisines in the world as well as one of the healthiest. None of that would make much difference if it wasn't one of the tastiest, too.

Like other cuisines of southeast Asia, Vietnamese cooking frequently incorporates four competing flavors—hot, sour, salty and sweet—into the same dish, resulting in a lively complexity. The dressing for papaya salad, for example, includes sour lime juice, sweet sugar, spicy chiles and salty fish sauce. Vietnamese cooking also features Chinese and French influences, thanks to China's long dominance of the region and France's shorter period as a colonial power. The sandwiches known as banh mis are made on baguettes spread with mayonnaise or butter and liver pâté, four ingredients not usually associated with Asian cooking. Another personal favorite, Vietnamese beef stew, is basically beef bourguignon with a fish sauce/ginger/anise cooking liquid taking the place of red wine.

Lots of uncooked ingredients are used, often for the texture they provide. Spring rolls—a kind of unfried egg roll—are packed with fresh lettuce, shredded carrot and fresh herbs. Asian cooks also prefer their protein as fresh as possible, which is why more seafood is sold live in their markets than in all the city's regular supermarkets put together.

The pungent liquid known as fish sauce is the glue that holds everything together, playing a role similar to soy sauce in Chinese cooking. An idea of its flavor profile can be surmised from its traditional method of preparation, which was to pack a wooden barrel full of anchovies and let it sit in the hot sun until a dark liquid began seeping out of the bottom—the fish sauce. Do *not* spill this stuff in your car. But do put it in any Vietnamese recipes that call for it or your dish will suffer. It's used as both an ingredient and table condiment, providing salty and umami elements to whatever you're making.

FRIENDS WITH BENEFITS

Not long after moving here, I made two great friends through writing about Vietnamese people and their food in Wichita. Minh Peng is a native of Laos but speaks Vietnamese and is known throughout the Asian community. She made numerous introductions for me and translated through language barriers. Plus, she's a fine cook in addition to possessing boundless enthusiasm and a seemingly inability to age.

One article I wrote with Minh's help—about the twenty-fifth anniversary of the Vietnamese immigration to Wichita—led to me being invited to a celebration held at St. Anthony Catholic Church in downtown Wichita, a center of the city's Catholic Vietnamese community. Cooks working in a half dozen rooms set up as makeshift kitchens cranked out course after course of Vietnamese delicacies. Surely, we sampled every Vietnamese dish known to man that night, I thought. Happily, I was wrong.

Minh Peng and her mother, Mui Peng, harvest produce from Mui's front-yard garden. *Photo by Annie Calovich.*

Danny Nguyen introduced himself the first time I ate at Pho Hot, the restaurant he owned at Pawnee and the Canal Route. Danny and I became friends right away. Or maybe it's more accurate to say that my wife and I became his groupies, trailing along as he moved his restaurant to Rock Road, where it was called Pho Hot Bistro, and then to Old Town, where it was rechristened Lemongrass Café.

I'm not sure what Danny thought of my incessant questions about Vietnamese

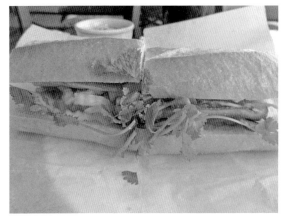

Left: Banh mi sandwiches are a delicious fusion of Vietnamese and French cuisines.

Right: Danny Nguyen visits with James Beard Award–winning chef Rick Moonen, who dined at Nguyen's restaurant during a book tour.

cooking, but he answered them all cheerfully, inviting me back into his kitchen to watch as he dispatched live blue crabs for a spicy stir-fry or skimmed a huge pot of pho to keep the broth clear. When a fresh shipment of crawfish or abalone or wild boar arrived, he'd call, and we'd come running. Danny has traveled widely and brought back cooking ideas from a lot of places, so some nights his specials veered into the realms of Cajun, French, Japanese or Korean cuisine. We were the beneficiaries. I know he appreciated our willingness to try anything, from fried pig ear to simmered cow intestine to a gelatin made primarily of blood (pig again). One night he took me up to the roof of his building in Old Town to sample kimchi and fermented shrimp he was making in mason jars set out in the hot sun. Meals with Danny routinely ran into the wee hours, generally accompanied by too much cognac.

Lemongrass was the city's most upscale Vietnamese restaurant. A health emergency forced Danny out of the restaurant business in 2019. He now works in a family business in Oklahoma, where he's set up a professional-grade kitchen in his garage, no doubt driving neighbors crazy with the fantastic aromas created there. If the food gods care about mortal tongues, he'll feed the wider public again someday.

*Saigon's No. 49

When I polled *Wichita Eagle* readers for the restaurant recipe they most desired, Saigon's No. 49 came out on top, one measure of how popular Vietnamese food is here. Owner Hanh Bui said the restaurant on North Broadway marinates the chicken overnight for this dish, but I found it tasted great when the chicken spent just five minutes in the marinade.

Makes 4 servings.

Source: Hanh Bui

½ cup hoisin sauce
2 tablespoons soy sauce
2 teaspoons minced garlic
½ teaspoon white pepper
1 ½ pounds chicken breast, cut into pieces about 1 inch by ½ inch by ¼ inch thick
½ pound rice vermicelli noodles
1 tablespoon oil
3 cups shredded lettuce
2 cups bean sprouts
½ cup chopped cilantro
¼ cup sliced green onion
4 tablespoons chopped peanuts

Sauce:
¼ cup lime juice
¼ cup fish sauce
¼ cup water
2 teaspoons rice vinegar
2 tablespoons sugar
1 jalapeño, chopped
Shredded carrot (optional)

Mix hoisin sauce, soy sauce, garlic and pepper. Place chicken in marinade while preparing vegetables and sauce. Make sauce by mixing lime juice, fish sauce, water, vinegar, sugar, jalapeño and carrot, if using. When ready to cook, prepare noodles according to package directions. Heat oil in a skillet or wok. Pour chicken and marinade into the skillet and stir-fry until done.

Among four bowls, divide lettuce, bean sprouts, cilantro, noodles, onion and chicken. Sprinkle with chopped peanuts and sauce and serve.

*Nuoc Cham

Jennifer Nguyen became known as the "Asian Answer Lady" while running the Asian Market on Central thanks to her ability to clear up confusion over ingredients and cooking techniques unfamiliar to some of her western shoppers (including this one). This is her recipe for nuoc cham, an all-purpose table sauce. Adjust the amount of each ingredient until you find the combination you like.
Source: Jennifer Nguyen

1 tablespoon fish sauce
1 teaspoon vinegar or lime juice
1 garlic clove, minced
1 red chili, seeded and finely chopped
2 teaspoons sugar
3 tablespoons water

Combine all ingredients in a bowl and mix well. Use as a dipping sauce or to pour over noodles and grilled meats.

*Spring Rolls

These healthy alternatives to fried egg rolls are a great start to any Vietnamese meal. The spring roll wrappers will seem too brittle to roll until they are softened in hot water. Many versions of these rolls use both shrimp and pork in the filling; fresh mint and basil, bean sprouts and shredded carrots also can be added.
Source: Jennifer Nguyen

2 ounces vermicelli noodles
2 cucumbers
1 pound cooked shrimp or pork
½ head lettuce
1 bunch cilantro, chopped
8 spring roll wrappers
Nuoc cham, for dipping

Soak noodles in hot water for 30 minutes or until al dente; drain, rinse in cold water and set aside. Alternately, they can be boiled for 2 to 3 minutes.

Peel cucumbers and remove seeds with a spoon. Slice thinly lengthwise. Halve the shrimp or chop the pork, if using. Shred lettuce.

Fill a large bowl with water that's hot, but not too hot to touch. Dredge a spring roll wrapper slowly through the water, submerging it completely for about 5 seconds. Lift it out, let any excess water drip off and transfer to a plate lined with paper towels. The wrapper will continue to soften somewhat.

In a line across the bottom third of the wrapper, layer 4 shrimp halves (or equivalent amount of pork), about 1 tablespoon noodles, several sprigs cilantro, several cucumber slices and ¼ cup chopped lettuce. Roll the spring roll up, folding in the sides as you would for a burrito.

Repeat with remaining ingredients and serve with nuoc cham or peanut sauce.

*Papaya Salad

This salad is another healthy appetizer or side dish—although it can be made less so with traditional garnishes of beef jerky and chopped peanuts. To turn it into an entrée, top with shrimp.

Source: Nga Nguyen, Lao Food Market

1 green papaya, about 2 pounds
1 jalapeño, seeded and minced
2 garlic cloves, minced
2 tablespoons fish sauce
Sugar, to taste
1 teaspoon lime juice
4 or 5 cherry tomatoes, halved

Peel papaya, cut in half lengthwise and scoop out seeds. Shred or chop papaya into matchstick-size pieces.

Mix papaya and other ingredients together and serve mounded on a plate.

*Café Sua

No trip to a Vietnamese restaurant is complete without café sua, an iced drink that provides a jolt of sugar and caffeine. It's traditionally made in a single-serving French press coffee maker, which can be bought for a few dollars in Asian markets along with the coffees called for in this recipe. When I asked Danny Nguyen for this recipe, he revealed that he also lightly sprays the ground coffee with Myers's Rum and Kahlua before brewing. No wonder his version is so tasty!
Source: Danny Nguyen

2 tablespoons Trung Nguyen brand coffee
1 tablespoon Café Du Monde brand coffee
Small pinch salt
Sweetened condensed milk, to taste

Combine coffees, salt and spoon into bottom of coffee maker. Fill a glass with ice and about ¼ to ⅓ cup sweetened condensed milk. Place coffee maker on top of glass.

Add just enough simmering water to come to top of coffee in coffee maker. Wait 3 minutes, then fill coffee maker to near top with more simmering water. Carefully screw plunger onto coffee maker, tightening it gently. When coffee finishes dripping, remove coffee maker from glass and stir contents together to combine.

Waiting for café sua to brew in a French press coffee maker is a happy ritual of dining in Vietnamese restaurants.

Spicy Garlic Chicken

Da Nang did brisk business as a tiny banh mi take-out shop on North Broadway but ran into problems after expanding. Even a glowing review by a visiting writer for the *New York Times* couldn't save it, proving that positive word of mouth is better than any publicity. But as this recipe from its later stage shows, its food remained excellent.

Source: Da Nang

2 chicken leg quarters (thighs and legs)
6 tablespoons oyster sauce
½ teaspoon black pepper
1 green bell pepper, cut into chunks
1 red bell pepper, cut into chunks
1 tablespoon vegetable oil
5 garlic cloves, minced
2–3 tablespoons ground red chili paste
Fresh cilantro sprigs, for garnish
6 cups steamed rice

Remove the meat from the leg quarters and cut into 1-inch pieces. Mix together 4 tablespoons oyster sauce and the black pepper. Pour over chicken and marinate in refrigerator at least 8 hours or overnight.

In a saucepan, boil the cubed bell pepper until slightly softened. Remove from water and set aside.

Heat oil in large skillet over medium-high heat. Add 4 minced garlic cloves and sauté until lightly browned (don't burn). Add chicken, stirring frequently. When nearly done, add bell pepper and cook 1 minute. Add remaining minced garlic clove, oyster sauce and ground chili paste and cook until heated through.

Garnish with cilantro sprig and serve over steamed rice with nuoc cham.

Beef Pho

You should be able to find soup bones (usually labeled marrow or knuckle bones) in your supermarket. If not, visit an Asian or Mexican market.
Source: Minh Peng

5 pounds beef soup bones
1 ½ pounds beef brisket
2 pounds oxtails
1 teaspoon salt
3 pieces star aniseed
2 pieces fructus amomi
1 2-inch piece ginger, sliced and smashed into chunks
2 onions, peeled and cut into fourths
1 tablespoon coriander seed, tied in cheesecloth
1 teaspoon sugar, or more to taste
1 teaspoon MSG
2 tablespoons fish sauce
1 package (14 ounces) pre-cooked meatballs (optional)
2 packages (16 ounces each) rice noodles
2 bunches cilantro, chopped
2 bunches green onions, chopped

Garnish:
Fresh basil or mint
Limes, cut into quarters
Bean sprouts
Sliced jalapeños

Place soup bones in large pot and cover with water. Bring to a boil, then pour off water and rinse bones well. Place bones back in pot with brisket, oxtails and salt. Add 7 quarts water. Bring to a boil, skimming off any scum that rises to the surface. Reduce heat to a simmer, continuing to skim as necessary.

Meanwhile, place star aniseed, fructus amomi, ginger and onion on a sheet pan. Broil in oven until onion is slightly charred. When cool enough to handle, add contents of sheet pan to soup pot with coriander.

Cook about 1 ½ hours or until brisket is done. Remove brisket from broth; wrap and refrigerate until ready to serve soup. Add sugar, MSG and fish sauce to broth.

Continue cooking for 3 to 4 hours, checking oxtail and removing when done (it should take about 1 hour longer than the brisket). You should have about 5 quarts water when done; add water if necessary due to evaporation. Remove coriander pouch. Broth can be prepared ahead to this point and refrigerated.

Before serving, strain broth and return to a low boil. Add meatballs, if using. Place rice noodles in warm water for 5 minutes while bringing a large pot of water to boil. Drain noodles and place in boiling water for 30 seconds. Drain noodles and divide among individual bowls.

Slice cooked brisket thinly and place in bowls. Add cilantro and green onion to bowls. Ladle broth and meatballs into bowls and serve with garnish plate.

Note: Star aniseed, fructus amomi, MSG, fish sauce, meatballs, bean sprouts and rice noodles are available at Asian markets. Some cooks add pho seasoning cubes or paste to their pho for additional flavor.

Chicken Pho

A small space across the parking lot from Thai Binh has housed a number of good restaurants through the years, including Café TuTu, whose chief cook, Mung Nguyen, provided this recipe. Chicken pho is lighter and cooks in a fraction of the time of the beef version, but it's still packed with flavor.

Makes 4 to 6 servings.

Source: Mung Nguyen

1 chicken, cut into eight pieces
8 cups water
1 onion, peeled and quartered
1 piece ginger, about 3 inches, slightly crushed
4 pieces star anise, or 1 teaspoon ground anise
3 cardamom pods
2 sticks cinnamon, or ½ teaspoon ground cinnamon
1 tablespoon fennel seeds
2 chicken bouillon cubes, if needed
About 1 tablespoon sugar
Salt, to taste
1 package rice noodles

1 bunch cilantro, chopped
1 bunch green onions, sliced

Optional garnishes:
Bean sprouts
Sliced jalapeño
Fresh basil leaves
Lime wedges

Cover chicken with water. Add onion, ginger, star anise, cardamom, cinnamon and fennel seeds. (If desired, you can tie everything but the onion and garlic in a cheesecloth sachet; if not, strain the broth later.) Bring mixture to a boil, then reduce heat and simmer chicken, uncovered, about 1 hour or until all pieces are tender. Skim off fat and impurities as they rise to the surface.

When the chicken is cooked, remove the pieces from the broth and allow to cool; then remove and discard bones and skin and chop the meat. Taste broth and bouillon if desired. Season to taste with sugar and salt. Pour broth through strainer or colander to remove onion, ginger, cinnamon sticks, etc. Return broth to heat.

Soak noodles in warm water for 5 minutes and drain. Bring a large pot of water to boil. Drop the noodles in boiling water and cook for 1 minute, then drain.

Serve pho by placing noodles in bowl followed by chicken meat, cilantro, green onions and broth. Serve with optional garnishes.

Thit Kho
Pho recipes can be intimidating. This soup—said to be as popular as pho in Vietnam—is much simpler. Wichita nurse Hang Pham, who provided it, said it's a dish traditionally made to celebrate the New Year but is so well liked that it's eaten year-round.
Source: Hang Pham

2 pounds pork butt or shoulder, cut into 1-inch pieces
4 tablespoons fish sauce
3 tablespoons vegetable oil
2 tablespoons sugar

3–6 cloves garlic, chopped
½ onion, chopped
I can (I4 ounces) coconut juice
4–8 eggs, hard-cooked and peeled

Mix together pork and fish sauce. Refrigerate for I hour.

In a heavy-bottomed pot, combine oil and sugar. Cook over medium heat, stirring frequently, until sugar turns to a brown liquid (do not burn). Add garlic and onion and cook for 30 seconds. Add pork pieces and fish sauce, stirring to coat with oil mixture, and cook 2 minutes. Add coconut juice and enough water to reach the top of the meat. Bring contents to a boil, then cover, reduce heat to simmer and cook until tender, about I ½ to 2 hours.

Halfway through cooking, add peeled, hard-cooked eggs to pot. Turn eggs once during cooking to color evenly.

Serve pork, cooking liquid and eggs accompanied by rice and pickled vegetables (recipe below).

Pickled Vegetables
Source: Hang Pham

⅓ cup vinegar
⅔ cup water
I teaspoon sugar
Dash salt
Several cups bean sprouts, green onions and carrots cut into thin strips

Mix vinegar, water, sugar and salt. Pour over vegetables and refrigerate. Serve with thit kho.

Goi Ga (Vietnamese Chicken Salad)
This light and healthy chicken salad is bursting with flavor thanks to the use of fresh garden herbs. It's delicious served warm, at room temperature or chilled.
Source: Minh Peng

Goi Ga, a popular Vietnamese chicken salad.

2 chicken breasts (1 to 1½ pounds),
cut into thirds
1 whole sweet onion, thinly sliced
2 tablespoons apple cider
5 tablespoons fish sauce, divided use
3 tablespoons sugar, divided use
4 tablespoons olive or vegetable oil, divided use
½ head of cabbage, thinly sliced
1 bunch (about 1 cup) cilantro, chopped
½ cup basil, chopped
½ cup mint (use more than one variety if
available)
5 tablespoons lemon juice
½ cup chopped peanuts
1–2 chile peppers, seeded and minced
(optional)

Boil chicken in water until done, about 10 minutes. Drain. When cool enough to handle, shred chicken with forks.

While chicken cooks, marinate onion for 15 minutes in apple cider, 2 tablespoons fish sauce, 1 tablespoon sugar and 2 tablespoons olive oil. Drain.

Combine chicken, cabbage and herbs in a large bowl. Make dressing by combining lemon juice, 3 tablespoons fish sauce, 2 tablespoons sugar and 2 tablespoons olive oil. Toss dressing with chicken, cabbage and herbs. Place on serving dish, garnish with chopped peanuts and minced chile, if using, and serve.

*Banh Mi

The small baguettes and cans of pâté traditionally used in making this sandwich can be found in Asian markets. In addition to grilled pork and chicken, fried eggs and cold cuts such as ham and head cheese are often used as fillings in banh mi.
Makes 6–8 sandwiches
Source: Danny Nguyen

Carrot-Daikon Relish:

½ pound carrots
½ pound daikon (an Asian radish available in many supermarkets)
1 ¼ cups vinegar
1 ½ cups water
1 ¼ cups sugar

Mini baguettes
Pâté
Mayonnaise
Grilled pork, sliced (see recipe below)
Cucumber slices
Cilantro sprigs
Jalapeño, chopped

To make relish, cut carrots and daikon into matchstick-size pieces. Marinate for 1 hour in mixture of vinegar, water and sugar; drain off liquid.

To make each banh mi, split baguette in half lengthwise and toast lightly. Spread thin layers of pâté and mayonnaise on lower level.

Top with slices of grilled pork, cucumber, cilantro, jalapeño and carrot-daikon relish.

Grilled Vietnamese Pork

Boneless chicken breasts or thighs can be substituted
for pork in this recipe.

Caramel sauce:

⅓ cup sugar
¼ cup fish sauce
4 shallots, sliced, or ¼ onion
Freshly ground black pepper

2 cloves garlic, minced
2 pounds boneless pork chops, cut into slices about 2 inches long and ¼ inch thick

To make caramel sauce: In a small heavy skillet or saucepan, cook sugar over low heat, stirring frequently, until brown. Remove from heat and stir in fish sauce, being careful to guard against splattering. Return mixture to heat and gently cook until sugar is completely dissolved. Remove from heat and add shallots and pepper.

Add garlic and pork to sauce. Allow to sit 30 minutes. Grill or sauté pork until done.

Clay Pot Salmon

Clay pots are esteemed for their ability to concentrate the flavor of foods cooked in them. A regular heavy-bottomed pot or skillet can be used with this recipe.
Source: Danny Nguyen

⅛ cup sugar
¼ cup vegetable oil
¼ cup fish sauce
Dash black soy sauce
Freshly cracked black pepper, to taste
1 pound salmon filets
2 scallions, chopped (white and green parts separated)
Water

In a clay pot or other cooking vessel, heat the sugar and oil over medium-high heat, stirring frequently, until sugar turns brown. Add fish sauce, stirring to combine, plus black soy sauce and pepper. Liquid in pot should be at a low boil. Using tongs, carefully lay salmon filets in skillet skin side down, then flip over so that all of fish is coated with liquid. Add white part of scallions and enough water to pot so that liquid comes to near the top of fish. Adjust heat if necessary so that liquid remains at a low boil without burning. Cook about 7 to 10 minutes or until fish easily flakes, carefully turning once. Remove fish from pot, garnish with green part of scallions and serve.

Note: Black soy sauce is a darker version of regular soy sauce. It's available in Asian markets. Dark or regular soy sauce can be substituted. This dish also can be made with boneless, skin-on catfish filets.

Fireman's Shrimp
Like ceviche, this spicy dish uses the acid in lime juice
to "cook" the shrimp.
Source: Danny Nguyen

1 tablespoon vegetable oil
1 large onion, sliced thin, divided use
1 pound raw shrimp, shell-on, 26–30 per pound size
Juice of 3–4 limes
⅛ cup sugar
⅛ cup fish sauce
⅛ cup sriracha, or to taste
¼ cup water
Fresh mint, minced
Finely chopped peanuts

Fireman's Shrimp gets its name from its spicy sauce, made with sriracha.

In a skillet, heat 1 tablespoon vegetable oil. Sauté three-fourths of sliced onion until lightly browned. Remove from heat and transfer onion to a non-metal pie pan or similar shallow dish.

Peel shrimp and remove dark digestive tract, if present. Butterfly each shrimp by cutting along the back curve, being careful not to cut all the way through, then spread out the two connected halves.

Place shrimp over sautéed onion in dish. Squeeze lime juice over shrimp and turn shrimp to make sure all pieces are in contact with lime juice. Cover with plastic wrap and refrigerate 30 minutes, turning shrimp once, or until shrimp are firm; one side will be white and the other red.

Remove shrimp from refrigerator and lightly squeeze with your hand to remove excess lime juice. Set aside. Repeat process with sautéed onion.

Spread sautéed onion along length of long, slender serving platter. Top with shrimp.

In a small bowl, combine sugar, fish sauce, sriracha and water. Drizzle over shrimp. Garnish with remaining sliced onion, mint and peanuts and serve.

Earthquake Beef
Source: Danny Nguyen

1 pound filet mignon, boneless ribeye or other steak
⅛ cup sugar
⅛ cup oyster sauce
Dash black soy sauce
1 tablespoon soy sauce
1 teaspoon sesame oil
Freshly cracked black pepper, to taste
Vegetable oil
½ each red and yellow bell pepper, cut into 1-inch chunks
1 yellow onion, cut into chunks

Cut beef into bite-size cubes. Place in a bowl or bag with sugar, oyster sauce, black soy sauce, regular soy sauce, sesame oil and black pepper. Marinate 30 minutes to 2 hours.

In a wok or large skillet, heat vegetable oil over medium-high heat. Add beef and marinade, cooking and stirring frequently, about 4 to 5 minutes or until desired doneness is reached. Add bell pepper and onion during last minute of cooking. If sauce seems too thick, add soy sauce.

Serve with rice.

Lemongrass Wings
Source: Danny Nguyen

12 chicken wings, separated at joint and wing
tips removed
1 tablespoon fish sauce
½ teaspoon MSG or chicken base (optional)
Cornstarch or tapioca flour

Sauce:
1 tablespoon chile oil
1 tablespoon minced lemongrass
1 tablespoon water
½ tablespoon fish sauce
½ tablespoon sugar
1 tablespoon butter

Danny Nguyen, a big fan of American football, concocted his Lemongrass Wing recipe for game days.

Rinse wings. In a large bowl, toss wings with fish sauce, MSG or chicken base if using and just enough cornstarch or tapioca flour to lightly coat them. Marinate at least 6 hours or overnight.

Deep fry wings at 350 degrees for 8 to 10 minutes or until crispy, golden brown and cooked through.

For sauce, combine all ingredients in a small saucepan and cook just until butter is melted.

Toss wings in hot sauce and serve.

PART III

DISHING WICHITA

Chapter 6

HOME ON THE RANGE

We had been feasting for hours. Or was it days? Bacon-wrapped dates stuffed with chorizo. A Caesar salad pungent with anchovy. A hunk of rare grilled beef. Rich baked pasta followed by even richer crème brûlée. All washed down with wines from three continents.

Which fine restaurant were we dining in? Actually, it was a friend's patio on a spring night in Wichita, hosts and guests each contributing courses.

My circle of talented home cooks expanded considerably after my wife, Carrie, arrived in town because—let's face it—she's a lot better company than I am. Suddenly we were being invited to all manner of people's homes for dinner and vice versa. Many became sources or subjects for my articles in the *Eagle*, *Splurge* and *Active Age*. Some became good friends.

Often, as we gazed over these tables spread with a frittata and mimosas for brunch or prime rib and martinis for dinner, we thought that we must be eating and drinking better than anybody in town. That's nonsense, of course, but it was sincere nonsense.

Did a little competition enter the equation when it was our turn to cook? Well, there was the 40-pound suckling pig we roasted for a summer party and the 1.5-pound, $135-lobe of foie gras we had shipped in on dry ice for a New Year's Eve celebration. As it turns out, we were pretty much the only fans of the latter, which was not a bad thing.

I love a good restaurant meal, don't get me wrong. The right server, food and ambience can add up to an amazing experience (with no dishes to wash!). But I'm a home cook at heart, just like the ones featured in this chapter.

Kathy Stark dishes up Green Chile in her east Wichita home.

No-Turn Grilled Salmon

Guy and Beth Bower are fun-loving forces on Wichita's food and wine scene. Both served as president of the American Institute of Food and Wine's local chapter and helped start its Midwest Winefest. Additionally, Guy hosts *The Good Life* on radio station KNSS, and Beth is a food writer. Don't expect stuffy talk about vintages and *velouté* sauce from the Bowers, who met in the military. Their approach can be summed up by Guy's go-to advice on wine: "Drink what you like."
Source: Guy Bower

Marinade:
Juice of 1 each: orange, lime, lemon
⅓ cup olive oil
⅓ cup dry white wine
⅓ cup mint, finely chopped
⅓ cup parsley, finely chopped
⅓ cup chives, finely chopped
2 cloves garlic, minced
1 tablespoon brown sugar

Vegetable oil
1 large Atlantic salmon filet, cut into individual portions

Combine marinade ingredients in a resealable bag. Place fish in bag and marinate 30 minutes (more time will make fish mushy).

Build a high-heat fire on one side of the grill. Clean the other side of the grill and rub with vegetable oil. Remove fish from marinade and place on cleaned side of grill. Cover and cook over indirect heat for 10 to 15 minutes or until golden brown and fish easily flakes. Do not turn.

Grilled Corn and Cherry Tomato Salad

Reverend Cindy Watson's ministry included teaching a class called "Joyous Cooking" at First United Methodist Church. This recipe joyously combines two summer treats—grilled corn and tomatoes—in a pretty salad.
Source: Cindy Watson

6 ears of corn
Olive oil, divided use
Salt and pepper
1–2 pints cherry tomatoes, quartered
2–3 scallions, sliced both white and green portions

Vinaigrette:
⅓ cup olive oil
3 tablespoons lime juice
1 clove garlic
½ to 1 teaspoon minced jalapeño
Salt and pepper, to taste

Like many good cooks, Cindy Watson keeps a vegetable garden in her backyard, located in the historic Midtown area.

Husk the corn and drizzle it with olive oil, salt and pepper. Grill over hot coals or over gas flames on medium-high until just beginning to brown on all sides. Let cool, then cut the corn kernels off the cobs.

In a bowl, whisk together olive oil, lime juice, garlic and jalapeño. Season to taste with salt and pepper. Combine the quartered cherry tomatoes, green onions and corn. Toss with the vinaigrette and serve.

Wagonmaster Smoked Brisket

I used to wonder if retired fire captain Bob Thompson might secretly be a pyromaniac, given his fondness for smoking meat. Thompson was happy to serve as firehouse cook early in his career with the fire department and later became lead cook for the Wagonmasters, the civic group/grown-up boys' club that raises money for Riverfest through various events. Since retirement, he's found a new gig cooking for Security 1st Title's corporate and charitable events.
Source: Bob Thompson

1 flat or point brisket, 2–4 pounds
Steak seasoning mixture (Thompson prefers the Montreal brand) or seasoned salt

Bob Thompson's cooking for Riverfest volunteers helped get him named the festival's ambassador, known as Admiral Windwagon Smith, in 2003. *Courtesy of Bob Thompson.*

Wash the brisket and pat dry. Rub brisket with steak seasoning. Wrap in plastic wrap and refrigerate several hours or overnight.

Start heating your smoker with charcoal and hickory wood or a fruitwood of your choice. (If possible, soak wood in water overnight.)

Place brisket in smoker and smoke for 2½ hours on one side. Turn brisket on the other side and smoke for another 2½ hours.

Remove brisket from smoker and wrap in aluminum foil. Return brisket to smoker and cook for an additional 2½ hours. Remove brisket from smoker, remove foil and let cool before slicing.

Note: Ideal temperature for smoking meat is 225 degrees. If you have a gas grill instead of a smoker, use the indirect heat method of cooking by setting the burner on one side on low and placing the brisket on the other side of the grill.

Crackling Corn Bread

A southern-style recipe from Bob Thompson, whose parents ran a café on Junction City's notorious Ninth Street. Note that the recipe calls for pork

cracklings, not rinds; the former have fat on the skin before they're fried, giving them a meatier taste. Thompson likes Mac's Cracklings sold at Wal-Mart.
Source: Bob Thompson

2 cups pork cracklings
1¼ cups cornmeal
¾ cup flour
¼ cup sugar
2 teaspoons baking powder
½ teaspoon salt
1½ cups buttermilk
¼ cup vegetable oil
1 egg, beaten

Coarsely grind pork cracklings in a food processor or blender. Set aside.
Heat oven to 400 degrees. Grease an 8- or 9-inch pan or 12-count muffin pan.
In a bowl, combine the ground cracklings with the dry ingredients. Stir in buttermilk, oil and egg. Pour batter into pan and bake 20 to 25 minutes or until light brown or a fork or toothpick inserted in the center comes out clean. Serve warm with honey.

Pear, Blue Cheese and Walnut Pizza
We've eaten so many great meals in the College Hill home of Deanna Harms and David Kamerer that it seems wrong to single out one. But here I go anyway.
Source: David Kamerer

Crust (makes two 12-inch crusts):
1 teaspoon sugar
1 cup warm water
1 teaspoon active dry yeast (or one packet)
About 2½ cups flour
1 teaspoon salt
3 tablespoons olive oil

David Kamerer and Deanna Harms are known for the easy elegance of their dinner parties. Here, David mans a vintage travel bar set up in their College Hill backyard. *Photo by Carrie Rengers.*

Topping (for one pizza):
Crumbled blue cheese
Shredded mozzarella cheese
1 ripe pear, sliced thin
English walnuts

Dissolve sugar in warm water. Put yeast in water and let bubble for a minute. Add 1 cup of flour and mix well. Add salt and oil.

Steadily add flour and continue mixing until dough cleans itself from sides of bowl. The actual amount of flour used varies according to humidity and other variables. Mix for an additional 10 minutes. (A quality stand mixer with dough hook greatly facilitates dough preparation.) Form dough into a ball, oil surface with 1 tablespoon olive oil, cover with a towel and put in a warm place to rise until doubled (about 45 minutes).

Preheat oven to 450 degrees. Divide crust into two equal pieces and punch down. Roll out on a floured surface to desired shape. Dust a cookie sheet with cornmeal and transfer crust. Top with blue cheese, mozzarella, thin pear slices and walnuts. Place in oven and bake until cheese just starts to brown, about 10 minutes. Unused dough can be sealed in a plastic bag and frozen for future use.

*Pastitsio

One bite of this Greek baked pasta dish and I had just one question: why had no one fed me this bit of heaven before? Calliope "Poppy" Toole, a cook for the annual bake sale at Holy Trinity Greek Orthodox Church, provided this recipe that I've made dozens of times since.
Source: Calliope Toole

2 pounds ground beef
2 medium yellow onions, chopped
½ bunch parsley, chopped
3 cups tomato sauce (one 15-ounce can and one 8-ounce can)
3 cups water
Salt and pepper, to taste
18 ounces uncooked pastitsio (Greek pasta) or elbow macaroni
1½ sticks butter, divided use
6 tablespoons fine bread crumbs, divided use
1¼ cups grated parmesan cheese, divided use
1 cup flour
4 cups milk
½ teaspoon nutmeg, or to taste
3 eggs, slightly beaten

Cook beef, onions and parsley together in a pot or large skillet until beef is brown and onions are translucent; drain off liquid.

Add tomato sauce and water to meat mixture; bring to a boil, then reduce heat and simmer, uncovered, about 1 hour or until liquid is nearly evaporated and mixture is thick, stirring occasionally. Season to taste with salt and pepper.

Meanwhile, cook pasta according to package directions; drain.

Melt 4 tablespoons butter. Brush the bottom and sides of a deep 9x13-inch lasagna pan with about 1 tablespoon of the butter. Add 3 tablespoons bread crumbs to the pan and tilt the pan until crumbs are evenly distributed around the bottom and sides (as you would while flouring a cake pan). Stir the remaining 3 tablespoons melted butter and ½ cup Parmesan cheese into the pasta.

Layer half the pasta in the bottom of the lasagna pan. Top with the meat mixture. Top the meat mixture with the remaining pasta.

To make the white sauce, cut 1 stick butter into 8 pieces. Place the butter, flour and milk in a saucepan. Heat, stirring constantly, over medium-high heat until mixture bubbles and thickens. Remove from heat. Add nutmeg. When mixture has cooled slightly, slowly stir in beaten eggs one at a time, making sure the heat does not curdle the eggs. Stir in ½ cup cheese.

Pour white sauce over pasta and meat layers. Top with remaining bread crumbs and Parmesan cheese.

Bake uncovered at 350 degrees for 1 ½ hours, or until golden brown. If the edges start to darken, cover the edges with aluminum foil.

*Bulgogi

Seventeen years after first writing about Domitilla Yu, a member of the Sisters of St. Joseph religious order, I reached her by telephone while putting together this book. "I'm still cooking," she said cheerfully. "In fact, I'm cooking right now!"

Source: Sister Domitilla Yu

3 pounds top round steak or similar cut of meat (see note below)
¼ cup sugar
⅓ cup soy sauce
2 teaspoons garlic, chopped
1 tablespoon white wine or sake
1 tablespoon sesame oil
½ teaspoon black pepper
2 teaspoons crushed beef bouillon
1 tablespoon sesame seeds
3 tablespoons green onion, chopped

Slice meat, against the grain, into thin strips. Sprinkle with sugar, then add soy sauce and remaining ingredients, stirring to coat evenly. Cover and marinate in the refrigerator for at least 5 hours.

When ready to cook, prepare charcoal or set gas grill on medium heat. Remove meat from marinade and grill strips for 1 to 2 minutes on each side, being careful not to overcook.

Note: I often make this dish with thin-cut beef short ribs, which are available in Mexican and Asian markets and occasionally show up in big-box stores.

Mandu (Korean Egg Rolls)
Source: Sister Domitilla Yu

1 pound ground beef
½ head cabbage, loose outer leaves and tough core removed
2 carrots, peeled and sliced into matchstick-size pieces
½ medium onion, chopped
1 egg
½ teaspoon garlic powder
1 tablespoon soy sauce
1 ½ teaspoons sesame oil
1 package egg roll wrappers
Vegetable oil, for frying

Brown beef in skillet; drain off fat.

Chop or shred cabbage. Place in large pot with carrots and several inches of salted water. Bring to a boil; remove pot from heat and drain vegetables. Run cold water over vegetables to prevent further cooking.

Mix together cooked beef, cabbage, carrots and remaining ingredients except for egg roll wrappers and oil.

Place 1 to 2 tablespoons of the filling just below center line of an egg roll wrapper and roll it according to package directions. Repeat with remaining ingredients.

Heat oil in skillet over medium heat. Fry egg rolls about 2 to 3 minutes per side or until golden brown.

Note: This mixture also can be used as a filling for wonton wrappers.

Dulce de Leche Apple Pie

Adriene Rathbun has been known to throw together dinner for six while guests are gathered around the table in her kitchen, drinks in hand. That kind of confidence comes from years of giving cooking classes in that same kitchen. Rathbun collected those recipes and more in a handsome cookbook called *Social Cooking*, which came out in 2020.
Source: Adriene Rathbun

Dulce de Leche Apple Pie. *Courtesy of Adriene Rathbun.*

½ cup brown sugar
⅓ cup granulated sugar
⅓ cup cornstarch
¼ teaspoon cinnamon
⅛ teaspoon freshly grated nutmeg
Pinch of salt
5 cups Granny Smith apples (about 5–7 apples, peeled and sliced)
¼ cup canned dulce de leche
2 tablespoons apple cider vinegar
½ teaspoon vanilla extract
Double pie crust

Place the oven rack on the lower third of the oven and preheat to 400 degrees.

Mix together sugars, cornstarch, cinnamon, nutmeg and salt. Make sure the cornstarch is mixed in well so you don't get cornstarch lumps in your pie.

In a large bowl, toss together the apples and dulce de leche, apple cider vinegar and vanilla extract. Add the dry mixture and toss to combine. Set aside.

Roll out the pie dough and stretch it about another inch or more for the bottom piece and roll the top piece gently to even out the dough.

Line a 9-inch pie dish with the bottom crust. Add filling and spread out evenly. Cut a few slits or cut out decorative cutouts in the top crust for venting. Cover with the top crust. Press the top dough into the bottom piece gently to stick together. Tuck the top edges into the pie dish, leaving a little crimp at the top. Pinch the edges.

Bake for 30 minutes. Then turn the temperature to 375 degrees. Cover the crust edges with either a pie guard or aluminum foil to create a shield. Bake for another 30 minutes or until crust is golden. Remove the pie from the oven and set on a cooling rack for several hours to set up the filling.

*Sweet and Spicy Lamb Lollipops

My friend Dana Britton and I often argue about who really won our one-and-only grilling competition (it was me), but I'll concede that this lamb recipe of his is a winner.

Source: Dana Britton

1 rack of lamb
½ cup soy sauce
½ cup sweet chile sauce (such as Mae Ploy or Maggi)

Use a sharp knife to separate rack of lamb into 8 chops. Place in shallow dish with soy sauce, turning to coat, and let marinate about 30 minutes.

When ready to cook, heat grill to medium-high. Grill lamb chops about 2 minutes per side, brushing with sweet chile sauce during last minute of cooking. Do not let chile sauce burn.

*Green Chile

Like many Wichitans, Kathy and Doug Stark regularly spend time in nearby New Mexico, drawn by its fine scenery, weather and food like this stew made by Kathy.

Source: Kathy Stark

2 tablespoons extra virgin olive oil
1 large white or yellow onion, chopped
2 pounds pork loin, cut into cubes
2 cloves garlic, minced
½ cup flour
8 cups chicken stock
1 can pinto beans, drained
1 tablespoon chile powder, preferably New Mexican
2 teaspoons ground cumin
2 cups mild to medium Hatch chiles, roasted, peeled and seeded
Salt and pepper, to taste

Heat olive oil in large Dutch oven over medium-high heat. Add onion and pork; sauté until pork is browned and onion is soft, adding garlic near end. Stir in flour, chicken stock, pinto beans, chile powder, cumin and chile peppers. Bring mixture to a boil, then reduce heat and simmer, covered, about I hour or until pork is tender. Season to taste with salt and pepper. Serve with tortilla chips, shredded cheese, sour cream and chopped cilantro if desired.

Pear Croustade with Lemon Pastry and Almonds

Lori Linenberger was my boss at the *Eagle* for several years. Despite that, she's still a friend—and a heck of a cook, as this dessert shows. If ripe pears are in short supply, you can substitute apples for half of them.
Source: Lori Linenberger

Pastry:
1 ½ cups all-purpose flour
2 tablespoons sugar
I teaspoon finely grated lemon peel
½ teaspoon salt
½ cup (1 stick) chilled unsalted butter, cut into ¼-inch slices
¼ cup (or more) whipping cream

Filling:
I pound firm but ripe Bartlett pears, peeled, cored, thinly sliced
I pound firm but ripe Bosc pears, peeled, cored, thinly sliced
5 tablespoons sugar
I tablespoon plus 2 teaspoons all-purpose flour
2 teaspoons fresh lemon juice
I teaspoon finely grated lemon peel
¼ teaspoon (generous) ground nutmeg
Whipping cream (for brushing)
2 tablespoons almonds, sliced
Vanilla ice cream (optional)

For pastry: Whisk flour, sugar, lemon peel and salt in a medium bowl. Add butter; using fingertips, rub in butter until coarse meal forms. Drizzle ¼ cup cream over; toss with fork until moist clumps form, adding more cream by teaspoonfuls as needed if dry. Gather dough into ball; flatten into disk. Wrap in plastic and chill I hour. (This can be made I day ahead.) Keep chilled. Let stand at room temperature 30 minutes before rolling out.

For filling: Preheat oven to 400 degrees. Mix all pears, sugar, flour, lemon juice, lemon peel and nutmeg in a large bowl to coat. Roll out pastry on a sheet of floured parchment paper to 14-inch round. Transfer crust on parchment paper to baking sheet. Mound pears in center of pastry, leaving 2-inch plain border. Fold pastry border over pears, crimping slightly. Brush pastry edges with cream; sprinkle with sliced almonds.

Bake croustade until filling bubbles and almonds are lightly toasted, about 1 hour. Cool slightly. Serve croustade warm or at room temperature with vanilla ice cream, if desired.

Cranberry Chocolate Chip Oatmeal Cookies

Peggy Smith, another former *Eagle* employee, told me that when she went to work there, it was expected that she would bring food to work because she was a woman. That's wrong, of course, but the treats Peggy brought for the newsroom were *soooo* right.

Source: Peggy Smith

2 sticks butter (1 cup)
1 cup brown sugar
½ cup white sugar
2 eggs
1¾ cups flour
1 teaspoon baking soda
1 teaspoon vanilla
1 teaspoon cinnamon
1 teaspoon pumpkin pie spice
3 cups oatmeal
1 cup mini chocolate chips
½ cup pecans, chopped
1 cup dried cranberries

Peggy Smith was the *Wichita Eagle*'s unofficial executive chef, organizing newsroom potlucks and regularly supplying co-workers with baked treats. *Photo by Brian Corn.*

Heat oven to 350 degrees. Cream butter and sugar. Add eggs. Mix well. Add flour, baking soda, vanilla and spices. Mix well. Add oats, chocolate chips, nuts and cranberries. Mix well.

Drop by cookie scoop or spoonful onto cookie sheet. Bake 10 to 12 minutes. Cool 2 to 3 minutes on cookie sheet and then transfer to a cooling rack.

Grilled Pizza Margherita

I met Don Hysko when Tanya Tandoc invited me over to see a guy cook pizza on her outdoor grill, then a fairly novel approach in these parts. Don, who had recently moved to town, proved just as exotic as the pizza with his heavy New England accent and one very long joke about quahogs (a type of clam). For a fun accompaniment to grilled pizza, see his wife Pat's Watermelon Salad recipe below.

Source: Don Hysko

1 package (3 pounds) frozen bread dough,
thawed according to package directions

Margherita sauce:
1 can (28 ounces) diced tomatoes
5 cloves garlic, chopped
4 tablespoons olive oil, plus additional olive oil for brushing dough
Salt and pepper, to taste

Topping:
Shredded cheese mixture for pizza (such as romano, parmesan and asiago)
Chopped basil

Separate each thawed loaf into three pieces, making nine pieces total. Brush pieces with olive oil, cover and allow to rise in a warm, draft-free location until double in volume.

Meanwhile, combine all sauce ingredients in a blender and process about 30 seconds, or until desired consistency is reached.

When ready to cook, prepare grill so that half of cooking surface is hot and the other is warm.

On a clean surface, stretch each piece of dough into a round shape 9 to 12 inches in diameter; they will be very thin. Place one crust on hot side of grill. As soon as it begins to puff up, about 30 seconds, begin picking up the edges and turning crust slightly. After another 30 seconds of cooking, turn crust over and place on cooler side of grill.

Brush crust with ¼ to ½ cup of sauce, sprinkle with cheese and basil and cook an additional minute. Remove and continue with remaining pizzas.

Watermelon Salad
Source: Pat Hysko

2 tablespoons white wine vinegar
1 lime, zested and juiced
¼ cup extra-virgin olive oil
Salt and pepper, to taste
1 red onion, thinly sliced
4 cups seeded watermelon chunks
1 cup crumbled feta cheese
¼ cup mint chiffonade (mint cut into thin strips)
2 cups baby arugula leaves

Pat Hysko is armed with gadgets for any job in the kitchen.

Stir together white wine vinegar, lime zest and juice in a small bowl. Whisk in olive oil and season with salt and pepper. Add thinly sliced onion and let marinate for 5 to 10 minutes as you prepare the rest of the salad.

Add watermelon, feta, mint and arugula to a large bowl. Toss with vinaigrette and serve immediately after dressing.

*Coconut Chicken Curry
Nidtaya Helms made beautiful salads and garnishes while working for the Wichita Country Club, but it was the cuisine of her native Thailand that I was most interested in learning about. This creamy curry comes together in minutes. Adjust the heat of the dish by using less or more curry paste. The Thai chile is for seasoning, not eating, unless you are accustomed to its heat.
Source: Nidtaya Helms

1 can coconut milk
1 tablespoon red curry paste, or to taste (see note)
1 pound chicken breast, cut into nugget-size pieces
1 heaping teaspoon sugar
1 basil leaf
1 red Thai chile
2 cups cooked rice

Put 2 tablespoons coconut milk in saucepan over medium heat. When it begins to spatter, stir in red curry paste until well blended.

Add chicken pieces and stir until coated. Add remaining coconut milk and sugar and bring to a boil. Reduce heat, cover and simmer about 8 minutes, until chicken is cooked. Turn off heat and add basil leaf and chile pepper to saucepan, allowing to steep for a minute. Serve over rice.

Note: Curry paste is sold in Asian markets and in the Asian sections of many supermarkets. Thai Kitchen is one brand that's widely available.

Embutido (Ground Pork Roll)

The annual Wichita Asian Festival is an event you must try at least once. You'll find food from India to Japan prepared by home cooks and sold for a pittance. This recipe was given to me by Rose Axman and Rosaline Quevedo, two sisters from the Philippines. With its filling of hard-cooked eggs and sausage, the meatloaf-like dish has great eye appeal when sliced.

This recipe makes 1 large or 2 smaller rolls.

Source: Rose Axman and Rosaline Quevedo

2½ cups ground pork
1 cup ground ham
½ cup onions, finely chopped
½ cup raisins
½ cup sweet pickles, finely chopped
½ cup green peas (thawed if using frozen)
1 cup grated cheddar cheese
2 eggs, hard-cooked and cut into quarters
4 Vienna sausages, cut into halves

In a bowl, mix pork, ham, onions, raisins, pickles, peas and cheese thoroughly.

Working with ¼ of mixture (if making 2 rolls), make a rectangular layer on a sheet of foil to form bottom of first roll.

Place half the egg quarters in a line down the center of the roll. Top with the sausage halves. Mound ¼ more of the pork mixture over egg and sausage pieces. Roll up the foil to create a log-shaped roll. Turn the roll and wrap it in another sheet of foil so that the roll is completely encased.

Repeat with remaining ingredients to form second roll. Place rolls in top of a covered steamer and cook 45 minutes. Or remove from foil, place in loaf pan and bake, covered, in oven at 400 degrees for 1 hour.

Roasted Red Pepper Soup

Nancy Blanchat has a flair for the dramatic in the kitchen—as in spectacular mishaps like dropping a tray full of flan moments before guests arrive. Her friends think it's all for show, though, because few others so consistently create such delectable dishes.

Source: Nancy Blanchat

Roasted Red Pepper Soup.

2 red bell peppers
1 onion, peeled and finely chopped
¼ cup butter
1 cup grated carrots
¼ cup flour
2 cups beef broth
2 cups half-and-half
1 can (15 ounces) tomato sauce
About ¼ teaspoon hot chile flakes, or to taste
Salt and pepper

Rinse the peppers and cut in half lengthwise. Remove and discard stems, seeds and veins. Lay peppers, cut side down, on a cookie sheet. Broil 4 to 6 inches from heat until skins are blackened all over, about 12 minutes. Remove from oven. When peppers are cool enough to handle, pull off and discard skins; chop peppers.

In a 3-quart pan over medium-high heat, sauté onion in butter until limp, about 3 minutes. Stir in peppers and grated carrots.

Add flour and stir about 1 minute. Add broth, half-and-half and tomato sauce; stir until mixture boils and is slightly thickened, about 10 minutes.

Stir in chile flakes and salt and pepper to taste and serve.

Cream-Filled Chocolate Cupcakes

Cooks across Wichita routinely volunteer their time, expertise and ingredients for good causes. Lucille Cline made these cupcakes for residents of the Ronald McDonald House near Wesley Medical Center. They taste like Ding Dongs without the plastic wrapping.
Source: Lucille Cline

Batter:
3 cups flour
½ cup cocoa
2 teaspoons baking soda
⅔ cup oil
2 cups sugar
1 teaspoon salt
2 tablespoons vinegar
2 cups cold water
2 teaspoons vanilla

Filling:
8 ounces cream cheese
1 egg
⅓ cup sugar
Dash salt
1 cup chocolate chips

Combine all batter ingredients. Fill each muffin tin with ¼ cup batter. To make filling, combine cream cheese, egg, sugar and salt, mixing well. Add chocolate chips and stir well.

Place 1 teaspoon filling mixture on top of batter in each muffin tin. Bake 20 minutes at 350 degrees.

Chimichurri
Chimichurri can be used as a marinade and/or sauce for meat. This recipe comes from Wichita businessman Jorge Della Costa, a native of Argentina, where chimichurri originated.
Source: Jorge Della Costa

2 tablespoons garlic, chopped
½ bunch parsley
½ tablespoon black pepper
1 teaspoon salt
½ teaspoon red pepper flakes
⅓ cup red wine vinegar
⅔ cup olive oil
1 tablespoon oregano

Combine all ingredients together in a bowl and let sit 2 to 3 hours before using.

Classic Tomato Pie
Angie Prather is best known for helping start the Wichita flag craze during her time with the Wichita Regional Chamber of Commerce. Friends say this savory pie starring fresh tomatoes, basil and cheese deserves just as much fanfare.
Source: Angie Prather

1 store-bought or homemade pie crust
2½ pounds tomatoes, sliced ¼ inch thick, lightly squeezed to remove seeds
2 teaspoons kosher salt, divided use
1 cup grated Gruyere cheese

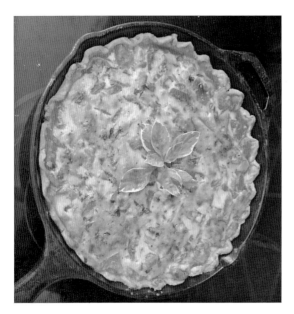

Classic Tomato Pie. *Courtesy of Angie Prather.*

1 cup shredded Monterey Jack cheese
¾ cup mayonnaise
1 large egg, lightly beaten
½ cup fresh basil, thinly sliced
1 tablespoon fresh thyme
¼ teaspoon freshly ground black pepper
1 cup red onion, chopped
Garnish: fresh thyme and basil, chopped

Press pie crust into bottom and up sides of a 10-inch cast-iron skillet. Crimp as desired. Refrigerate for 30 minutes.

Place tomato slices on paper towels; sprinkle with 1 teaspoon salt. Let stand at room temperature for 30 minutes. Preheat oven to 425 degrees.

In a medium bowl, stir together cheeses, mayonnaise, egg, basil, thyme, pepper and remaining 1 teaspoon salt.

Sprinkle red onion over prepared crust; top with one-third of cheese mixture. Layer half of tomatoes in an overlapping pattern; top with one-third of cheese mixture. Repeat with remaining tomatoes and remaining cheese mixture.

Bake until golden brown and center is set, 40 to 45 minutes. Let cool completely. Garnish with basil and thyme, if desired.

*Asparagus with Easy Aioli

Williams-Sonoma employee Barbara Flynn shared this recipe. The ice water bath is key to success; it will keep the asparagus crisp. I like adding a little lemon juice to the aioli.

Source: Barbara Flynn

1 bunch asparagus, trimmed
4 cloves garlic, minced
½ cup mayonnaise

Fill a bowl with ice water while bringing a pot of salted water to boil. Blanch asparagus in boiling water about 2 to 3 minutes or until the tip of a fingernail easily pierces asparagus. Remove asparagus from heat, drain and place in ice water until cool; drain on paper towels. Asparagus should be al dente, or firm enough to stand up when placed in a glass.

Meanwhile, stir garlic into mayonnaise.

Serve mayonnaise-garlic mixture alongside asparagus.

Catfish Cantonese

City employee Lewis Lau impressed with this dish, which uses a light dusting of cornstarch to create a crisp crust for the fish and tangerine peel to brighten the sauce.

Source: Lewis Lau

2 pounds catfish fillets
4 tablespoons soy sauce, divided use
1 teaspoon cooking wine
1 teaspoon sesame oil, divided use
Cornstarch
3 tablespoons corn oil, divided use
4 Chinese mushrooms, rehydrated (if using dried) and chopped
2 tangerine peels (orange part) or 1 orange peel, shredded
1 teaspoon sugar
2 dashes white pepper
3 tablespoons water

1 tablespoon oyster sauce
2 green onions, chopped

Marinate fish for 5 minutes in mixture of 2 tablespoons soy sauce, cooking wine and ½ teaspoon sesame oil. Dust with cornstarch, then fry in 2 tablespoons of corn oil until golden brown. Remove from skillet and keep warm. In clean skillet, add 1 tablespoon corn oil and stir-fry mushrooms and shredded peel. Stir in 2 tablespoons soy sauce, sugar, ½ teaspoon sesame oil, white pepper, water, oyster sauce and dash of cornstarch. Pour sauce over fish and serve garnished with onions.

Black Bean Pumpkin Soup

Best of Times owner Nancy Robinson jokes that she could do public relations (her former career) for soup in general. This one needs no hype; made for a cool fall day, it's healthy and hearty enough to serve as a main course.

Source: Nancy Robinson

3 cans (15.5 ounces each) black beans, rinsed and drained
1 cup drained canned tomatoes, chopped
1 ¼ cups chopped onion
½ cup minced shallots
4 garlic cloves, minced
1–2 teaspoons ground cumin
1 teaspoon salt
½ teaspoon pepper
½ stick butter
4 cups beef broth
1 can (16 ounces) pumpkin puree
½ cup dry sherry, plus 2 tablespoons, divided use
½ pound cooked ham, cut into ½-inch dice
2 tablespoons white vinegar
Optional garnishes: croutons, sour cream, lightly toasted pumpkin seeds

Puree beans and tomatoes. In a 6-quart kettle, cook onion, shallots, garlic, cumin, salt and pepper in butter over moderate heat, stirring until onion is softened and beginning to brown. Stir in bean puree.

After a hard day of retailing, business owner Nancy Robinson warms up with a bowl of Black Bean Pumpkin Soup.

Stir in broth, pumpkin and ½ cup sherry until combined and simmer, uncovered, stirring occasionally, for 25 minutes. Just before serving, add ham, vinegar and remaining sherry, stirring until heated through. Makes 10 cups.

Arrozo con Gandules (Rice and Peas)

Elizabeth Brunscheen-Cartagena, a family nutritionist at the Sedgwick County Extension Center, draws on fond memories of growing up in Puerto Rico when feeding her own family. Like many Puerto Rican dishes, Arrozo con Grandules starts with the aromatic mixture known as sofrito (see next recipe). The optional banana leaves, available in Hispanic markets, give the rice a slightly smoky flavor.
Source: Elizabeth Brunscheen-Cartagena

3 tablespoons vegetable oil
1 can (16 ounces) tomato sauce
½ cup sofrito
1 packet from a 1.41-ounce box of Sazon seasoning with achiote (available in Hispanic aisle of supermarkets)
2 cups long-grain rice
4–5 cups hot water
1 can (16 ounces) pigeon peas (available in Hispanic markets and some supermarkets)
Salt and pepper, to taste
Banana leaves (optional)

In a medium pot, combine oil, tomato sauce, sofrito and Sazon. Cook over medium heat for 4 minutes.

Add remaining ingredients except for banana leaves, including enough hot water to cover the rice by 1 inch. Bring to a boil and cook over high heat until most of the water is absorbed. Once water has been absorbed, stir from bottom to top once or twice. Lay banana leaves over rice, reduce heat to low, cover pot and continue cooking for about 30 minutes or until rice is tender. Remove banana leaves and discard before serving rice.

Sofrito
Makes about 3 cups.
Source: Elizabeth Brunscheen-Cartagena

1 large onion
1 large bell pepper
1 medium head garlic
1 bunch cilantro
1 small jar pimientos (roasted red peppers)
¼ cup olives
1 tablespoon capers
2 teaspoons salt
1 tablespoon black pepper
1 tablespoon crushed oregano
½ cup olive oil

Chop onion, bell pepper, garlic, cilantro, pimientos, olives and capers. Place in blender or food processor with remaining ingredients and puree.
Store in a covered glass jar in the refrigerator or freeze in ice cube trays and store cubes in freezer bags.

Chicken Taco Casserole
The Derby Senior Center is one of the biggest and busiest in the area, partly due to meals like this one prepared by volunteer Sharon Davidson. The former realtor also cooked meals for up to ninety at her church, First Presbyterian of Derby.
Source: Sharon Davidson

4 cups shredded cooked chicken
2 cans (10¾ ounces each) condensed cream of chicken soup
1 cup sour cream
1 can (10 ounces) diced tomatoes with green chiles, undrained
1 can (about 15 ounces) black beans, rinsed and drained
1 package (about 1 ounce) taco seasoning mix
5 cups coarsely crushed tortilla chips
2 cups shredded cheddar cheese

Cooking for crowds doesn't faze Sharon Davidson, thanks to recipes such as Chicken Taco Casserole.

Mix chicken, soup, sour cream, tomatoes, black beans and taco seasoning together. Spread half the mixture into the bottom of a greased 13x9-inch pan. Sprinkle 3 cups of the crushed chips over the mixture, then cover the chips with 1 cup of the shredded cheese.

Layer the remaining chicken mixture and top with the rest of the crushed chips. When ready to cook, cover and bake 30 minutes in a preheated 350-degree oven. Uncover, sprinkle the rest of the cheese over the top and bake an additional 10 minutes or until the cheese is melted.

Lucky guests at one dinner party still talk about the sauce Jackie Smith spent three days perfecting. Her recipe for Asparagus with Fried Eggs, Pancetta and Parmesan, on the other hand, comes together quickly.

Asparagus with Fried Eggs, Pancetta and Parmesan

Jackie Smith is something of a legend for dinner party fundraisers she and her husband, John, throw at their east-side home. Willing to spend days on a recipe when required, she's just as comfortable improvising a dinner for four like this with ingredients she has on hand.
Source: Jackie Smith

Vinaigrette:
1 teaspoon Dijon mustard
¼ cup white wine or champagne vinegar
1 cup extra-virgin olive oil
Salt and pepper, to taste

12 slices pancetta, torn into pieces (bacon can be substituted)
2 bunches asparagus, washed and ends trimmed
Kosher salt and freshly cracked black pepper
8 eggs
About ½ cup shaved parmesan cheese

For vinaigrette, whisk mustard and vinegar in a small bowl. Slowly whisk in olive oil. Add salt and pepper to taste.

Fry pancetta in large, nonstick skillet until crisp. Drain on paper towels, saving fat from the skillet.

Cook asparagus in a steamer to desired doneness (it can also be roasted, boiled or grilled). Set aside and season lightly with salt and pepper.

In the skillet, fry eggs in rendered pancetta fat over medium-high heat until whites are set and yolks are still slightly runny. Season to taste.

To prepare: Divide asparagus into 4 servings and place on warmed plates. Top each with two fried eggs and pancetta. Drizzle with vinaigrette. Top with shaved parmesan. Serve with crusty bread.

Chicken Florentine

Known for being tough on criminals while serving as Sedgwick County district attorney, Nola Foulston has a soft spot for anything Italian thanks to growing up in a large Italian-American family on the East Coast.
Source: Nola Foulston

3 eggs, yolks and whites separated
6 boneless, skinless chicken breasts
Italian-style bread crumbs (such as Progresso)
Olive oil
1 package frozen chopped spinach, thawed
Pinch pumpkin seasoning or nutmeg
1 ball fresh mozzarella cheese, sliced ¼ inch thick
Tomato sauce, homemade or store-bought

Beat egg whites until soft peaks form. Dip chicken breasts in egg whites, then coat on both sides with bread crumbs.

Heat olive oil in skillet over medium heat and cook chicken until golden brown, about 3 minutes on each side.

Meanwhile, squeeze water out of spinach. Combine with 3 egg yolks and pumpkin spice.

Top chicken breasts with spinach mixture and slices of cheese. Reduce heat to low and cover skillet. Continue cooking about 5 minutes, or until chicken is cooked through.

Serve with tomato sauce.

Winfield Camp Beans

Food is nearly as important as music to some of the campers who return to Winfield each fall for the Walnut Valley Festival. Some people have been camping together for decades, each taking turns cooking for the group. Naturally, dishes like this that feed a crowd are popular.

Source: Shalen Scheltgen

1 pound ground beef
10 slices bacon, chopped
½ cup onion, chopped
⅓ cup brown sugar
¼ cup ketchup
¼ cup barbecue sauce
2 tablespoons prepared mustard
2 tablespoons molasses
½ teaspoon salt
½ teaspoon chile powder
½ teaspoon black pepper
1 can (16 ounces) each kidney beans, butter beans, black beans
and pork and beans

Cook beef, bacon and onion in deep saucepan until beef is brown; drain grease. Stir in remaining ingredients except beans; mix well.

Add beans and pour into slow cooker. Cover and cook on low 5 to 6 hours.

Harry Pape was an early adopter of grilling romaine, which deepens the lettuce's flavor. To grill romaine, cut the head in half lengthwise, drizzle with olive oil and season with salt and pepper. Grill both sides until leaves wilt and grill marks appear. Serve with vinaigrette or other dressing. Pape is the author of *Simple Cooking with Chef H* and one of my fellow culinary instructors at Mark Arts.

Tiramisu

Tim Churchill plays Santa for kids at McConnell Air Force Base. His tiramisu recipe is a gift for cooks in a hurry since it sets up quicker than those calling for raw eggs. For a lighter version, add 8 ounces of frozen whipped topping to the filling.

Source: Tim Churchill

Filling:

2 packages (8 ounces each) mascarpone cheese at room temperature
1 package (8 ounces) cream cheese at room temperature
1 tablespoon instant espresso powder
2 tablespoons rum or almond-flavored liqueur (optional)
1 cup powdered sugar
2 teaspoons vanilla

Layers:

1 tablespoon rum or almond-flavored liqueur (optional)
2 cups strong coffee, cold
2 packages (or about 6 ounces total) crispy ladyfinger cookies
Cocoa powder

To make filling, mix ingredients until smooth.

Before assembling, add liqueur to coffee, if using. To assemble, take a ladyfinger and dip quickly in the cold coffee. Place in bottom of serving dish. Repeat with cookies, using about half the package, until bottom of pan is filled.

Spread half of filling mixture over cookies. Dust with cocoa powder. Repeat with remaining cookies, coffee mixture and filling. Dust top with cocoa powder and chill 1 to 2 hours before serving.

Green Chicken Chili

Tricia Holmes isn't likely to run out of the chile verde called for in this recipe. Her family makes it and other products under the Holmes Made label, an extension of the family produce business dating back to 1924.

Source: Tricia Holmes

1 cooked rotisserie chicken, skinned and boned
2 cups mild or medium roasted green chiles, stemmed, skinned and seeded
4 cups chicken broth
4 cans (15 ounces each) Northern white beans, undrained
1 jar (16 ounces) chile verde or salsa verde
1 tablespoon minced garlic
1 tablespoon dried parsley
1 tablespoon dried basil
1 tablespoon ground cumin
1 teaspoon salt, or to taste

Shred chicken by hand. Finely chop or grind green chiles in a food processor. Place chicken, green chiles and broth in a crockpot or stovetop pan. Add 2 cans white beans and mash with a masher. Add the other 2 cans of beans, leaving them whole. Add chile verde and spices and cook mixture until ingredients are hot and flavors are blended. Serve in a bowl garnished with shredded Monterey Jack cheese, sour cream and chopped cilantro.

Note: Chile verde can refer either to a salsa made with chiles and tomatillos or to a stew made with chiles and pork. This recipe calls for the former, which is also known as salsa verde.

Fried Plantains (Tostones)

Wichita elected two mayors in a row who were crack cooks: Carlos Mayans, who served from 2003 to 2007, and Carl Brewer, who served from 2007 to 2015. Mayans, a native of Cuba, immigrated to Kansas as a thirteen-year-old following the Communist takeover of that country. Here's his recipe for fried green plantains, a staple of Caribbean cooking. The method of frying them twice transforms them into a delicious snack or side dish.
Source: Carlos Mayans

Green plantains (available in Hispanic and Asian markets
and some supermarkets)
Vegetable oil, for frying
Salt

Cut ends from plantains. Make one slit along length of peel. While holding plantain under cold running water, ease off the peel.

Slice plantains into 1-inch-thick rounds. Cook in hot oil 2 to 3 minutes, turning over midway.

Remove from oil with slotted spoon and place on double layer of waxed paper. Press down on plantains with flat bottom of jar until about ¼ inch thick.

Return to hot oil and cook until golden brown and crispy on the edges. Drain on paper towels and sprinkle with salt.

Hizzoner's Ribs

It takes a confident politician to market a barbecue sauce with a picture of a bull on the bottle. Then again, the late Carl Brewer won election as Wichita mayor twice by easy margins. Had a few more voters had the chance to sample Brewer's cooking, he might have succeeded in his 2018 run for governor.
Source: Carl Brewer

The late mayor Carl Brewer was known for his easygoing personality and barbecue expertise.

Rub:

1 cup brown sugar
2 tablespoons chile powder
2 tablespoons dry mustard
2 tablespoons onion powder
2 tablespoons garlic powder
2 tablespoons cayenne pepper
2 tablespoons sea salt
2 tablespoons ground black pepper
Optional: barbecue sauce, butter, honey

1 rack ribs (baby back, spare or St. Louis style)

For rub, combine all ingredients. Makes about 2 cups. Can be stored indefinitely in an airtight container.

To smoke ribs: Remove thin membrane from ribs, if present. Season generously with rub (about 1 tablespoon per pound of meat).

Cook ribs over low (225 to 250 degrees), indirect heat, 4 to 6 hours for a 3-pound slab of ribs. For added flavor, brush with butter and honey near end of cooking time. When done, wrap ribs in foil and allow to rest 30 minutes before slicing. If desired, brush with a mixture of equal parts barbecue sauce, butter and honey just before serving.

Warm Spinach Salad

If a salad can be comfort food, this one qualifies with its warm dressing coating spinach, bacon, mushrooms and eggs. Lulu Moore had spent a lifetime cooking by the time I met her, but the retired caterer admitted she'd still jump up in the middle of the night to get meals ready for her church, Tabernacle Church of God in Christ.

Source: Lulu Moore

1 pound fresh spinach
2 cups mushrooms, sliced
1 cup water chestnuts, sliced
4 hard-cooked eggs, sliced
4 slices bacon
⅓ cup vegetable oil
¼ cup sugar
¼ cup ketchup
¼ cup vinegar
2 tablespoons Worcestershire sauce

Wash spinach; remove stems and tear leaves into bite-size pieces (skip latter two steps if using baby spinach). Combine in large bowl with mushrooms, water chestnuts and hard-cooked eggs.

In pan, cook bacon until fat is rendered and bacon is crisp. Remove bacon and add vegetable oil, sugar, ketchup, vinegar and Worcestershire sauce to fat. Stir to mix and bring to a boil. Remove from heat and pour over spinach mixture, tossing lightly to coat. If desired, crumble cooked bacon and add to salad.

Cheese-Filled Focaccia with Herbs

Teresa Lang spent twenty years as a Sedgwick County food extension agent, talking many a resident through Thanksgiving dinner preparation and other challenges. (Favorite question: "Can you defrost a turkey in the toilet and flush it every twenty minutes?") This recipe makes good use of the Kansas Grown Farmers Market held on Saturdays at the Extension Center, 21st and Ridge.

Source: Teresa Lang

2 loaves frozen bread dough, 1 pound each, thawed (do not let rise)
2 tablespoons olive oil
6 ounces Provolone cheese, grated
6 ounces Jarlsberg cheese, grated
4 tablespoons fresh basil (2 teaspoons dried)
1 tablespoon fresh oregano (½ teaspoon dried)
1 tablespoon fresh marjoram (½ teaspoon dried)
1 tablespoon fresh rosemary (½ teaspoon dried)
2 cloves garlic, finely minced
¼ cup Parmesan cheese, freshly grated

On a floured surface, roll 1 loaf of thawed dough into a 10x15-inch rectangle. If dough shrinks back after rolling, let it rest for a few minutes, then continue rolling to correct size. Transfer dough to a greased 10x15-inch jellyroll pan. Press dough to fit into corners.

Brush dough with 1 tablespoon olive oil. Cover with Provolone and Jarlsberg cheeses. Sprinkle with half the basil and top with oregano, marjoram, rosemary and minced garlic.

On a lightly floured surface, roll out second thawed loaf of dough into a 10x15-inch rectangle. Place on top of cheese and herbs. Pinch edges of bottom crust of dough to top and seal. Brush top of dough with remaining 1 tablespoon of olive oil and let rise until puffy, 30 to 60 minutes.

Heat oven to 375 degrees. Before baking, make dimples in the dough with fingertips or wooden spoon handle. Sprinkle dough with Parmesan cheese and remaining basil. Bake 25 to 30 minutes or until crust is golden brown and sounds hollow when tapped. Immediately remove from pan to cool on wire rack. Slice into strips or squares and serve warm.

New Year's Day Crepes

Carter Green says the key to tender crepes is preparing the batter the
night before—in his case, on New Year's Eve.

Source: Carter Green

4 eggs
1 ½ cups milk
1 cup water
2 cups flour
6 tablespoons melted butter, plus more for cooking crepes

Fillings:

Smoked salmon
Cream cheese
Slice bananas
Nutella
Peanut butter
Whipped cream
Berries
Powdered sugar

Carter Green,
a recording
studio
owner and
Francophile,
has made
a ritual of
serving crepes
and mimosas
to friends and
family on the
first day of
the year.

Mix eggs, milk, water, flour and 6 tablespoons butter in blender for 30 seconds. Refrigerate batter overnight.

When ready to cook, stir batter once while melting 1 teaspoon butter in crepe pan or nonstick skillet set over medium heat. Pour in ¼ to ⅓ cup batter and swirl around to fill pan evenly. Cook about 1 to 2 minutes or until batter appears set. Flip crepe over and cook about 30 seconds. Repeat with remaining batter, adding butter to pan as needed.

Serve crepes warm or at room temperature with fillings.

Chicken Salad in Wonton Boats

These are classic hand-held appetizers for the kind of party Ruthie McLain likes to throw. They're handy for hostesses, too, since the components can be prepared in advance. Spoon the chicken salad into the wonton boats just before serving to avoid the latter becoming soggy.

Source: Ruthie McLain

1 package wonton wrappers
4 cups cooked, diced chicken
1 cup Granny Smith apple, peeled and chopped
1 cup celery, chopped
1 cup mayonnaise
1 small can Mandarin oranges, drained and chopped
½ cup walnuts, chopped

Preheat oven to 325 degrees. Brush one side of wonton wrappers with vegetable oil and place in tartlet tins or mini muffin cups. Bake about 12 minutes, or until golden brown. Remove from oven and cool.

Combine chicken, apple, celery, mayonnaise, oranges and walnuts. Divide between wonton boats and serve.

Apple Strudel

My first boss at the *Eagle*, Tom Schaefer, cautioned me that I'd be covering a lot of church (and synagogue and temple and mosque) dinners if I took the job. Happily, he turned out to be right. Paula Van Andel, a member of Congregation Emanu-El, was typical of the cooks who put their talents to work in these events, baking this for the congregation's Deli Day.

Makes about 2 dozen pieces

Source: Paula Van Andel

2 sticks butter
1 cup sour cream
2 cups flour
Vegetable oil
1 ½ cups raisins
1 ½ cups chopped nuts
3 cups cooked apples or 1 can (24 ounces) apple pie filling
1 cup bread crumbs
2 tablespoons apricot preserves
2 tablespoons lemon rind, grated
Cinnamon and sugar

One day ahead, make dough. Cream butter, sour cream and flour. Batter will be sticky. Chill in refrigerator overnight.

Preheat oven to 400 degrees. Divide dough into three balls. Roll each between palms to form long bread sticks. With a rolling pin, roll each stick out on a floured board into thin, oblong shapes. Brush oil over entire surface of dough. Down the center of each piece, sprinkle with a combination of the raisins, nuts, apples and bread crumbs, then top with apricot preserves. Over that, sprinkle lemon rind. Roll up and seal ends; pat down slightly. Brush oil over entire surface; sprinkle with cinnamon and sugar.

Grease pan with oil or line with parchment. Bake at 400 degrees for 20 minutes. Cut each strudel into 1-inch slices while hot.

Goat Cheese and Sun-Dried Tomato Torte

This appetizer combines three of my favorite things: goat cheese, pesto and sundried tomatoes. Randalea Hinman prepared it for guests on a tour of historic Midtown homes.

Source: Randalea Hinman

8 ounces cream cheese, softened
12 ounces Montrachet goat cheese
½ pound (2 sticks) butter, softened
1 cup basil pesto
1 cup sun-dried tomatoes, drained and minced

Place cheeses and butter in a bowl and beat together until they are well blended and fluffy. Line an 8-inch cake pan with dampened cheesecloth, leaving enough extra to fold over the top.

Layer one-third of the cheese mixture in the bottom and spread half the pesto over it. Repeat. Spread remaining cheese on top and cover with the minced tomatoes.

Place a piece of plastic wrap over the top and fold the cheesecloth over it. Set the torte in the refrigerator for at least an hour to firm up. When ready to serve, fold the cheesecake back, turn the torte onto a plate and remove the cheesecloth. Invert the torte onto a serving plate and remove the plastic wrap. Serve with assorted crackers.

Biscotti

Shelly Thurman-Wing was one of my students in Butler Community College's culinary program, but there was little I could teach her about baking. Twice as old as most of the students, "Mom" (as they called Shelly) was voted MVP of her class. She went on to start a baking business in Cheney.

Source: Shelly Thurman-Wing

3½ cups all-purpose flour
1 cup whole wheat flour
2 tablespoons instant espresso powder
2 tablespoons coffee beans, coarsely ground
2 teaspoons baking powder

Shelly Thurman-Wing earned a culinary degree from Butler Community College after a long career with Coleman.

½ teaspoon baking soda
½ teaspoon salt
2½ cups slivered almonds
¾ cup light brown sugar, packed
½ cup granulated sugar, plus more for sprinkling
I teaspoon grated lemon zest
I teaspoon grated orange zest
4 large eggs
I cup vegetable oil
½ teaspoon vanilla extract
I teaspoon almond extract
I teaspoon egg wash, or as needed (see note)

Preheat oven to 350 degrees.

In a mixing bowl, whisk together flours, espresso powder, coffee beans, baking powder, baking soda, salt and almonds. Set mixture aside.

In the bowl of an electric mixer using the paddle attachment, blend the two sugars, the zest and the eggs on medium speed until the mixture is slightly thickened.

On low speed, gradually add the oil and vanilla and almond extracts. Still on low speed, add the dry ingredients and blend until just combined.

Divide the dough in half and form each half into a log about 15 inches long by 3½ inches wide. Place each log on a sheet pan lined with parchment paper.

Brush each log with egg wash and sprinkle generously with granulated sugar. Bake about 30 to 32 minutes or until the logs are firm but have little color. The top of the logs should look cracked.

Allow the logs to cool 5 to 10 minutes. Then, using a serrated knife, slice each log crosswise into slices about ¾ inch thick. Place the slices cut side down on the same sheet pan.

Return the slices to the oven and bake 6 to 8 minutes on each side. Cool completely. For extra sweetness and presentation points, dip the slices partially into melted dark and/or white chocolate.

Note: To make egg wash, whisk together I egg and I tablespoon water.

Purple People Corn Dip

Wichitans love a good tailgate, from high school games on up. More than a few take part in pre-game festivities at Arrowhead Stadium in Kansas City, generally ranked as the top tailgating destination in the country. As its name implies, this recipe comes from a K-State fan.
Source: Brenda Compton

8 ounces cream cheese
1 cup sour cream
¼ cup mayonnaise
¼ teaspoon garlic salt
½ teaspoon Tabasco or other hot sauce
½ teaspoon salt
8 strips bacon, fried and crumbled, or 1 jar bacon pieces
8 ounces corn niblets, drained (can use Mexicorn if desired)

Combine all ingredients and refrigerate at least 8 hours or overnight. Serve with corn chips.

Souvlaki

As a small businessman, Evangelos Nantsis told me, he couldn't pay employees of his computer recycling operation as much as he'd like. He tried to make up for it with once-a-month staff meals like this from his native Greece, prepared on a grill in the parking lot.
Source: Evangelos Nantsis

3 pounds pork tenderloin, beef steak, boneless chicken or lamb
⅓ cup olive oil, plus a little more for brushing the pita loaves
1 tablespoon minced garlic
½ tablespoon dried oregano
Salt and pepper, to taste
Metal or wooden skewers
Salt, to taste
8–10 pita loaves
Red onion, chopped

Tomatoes, diced
Tzatziki sauce (see next recipe)

Trim fat from meat and cut meat into 1½-inch chunks. Place in a bowl or resealable plastic bag. Add olive oil, garlic, oregano and pepper. Toss to coat evenly. Refrigerate, covered, at least 8 hours or overnight.

Remove meat from refrigerator and discard marinade. Thread meat onto skewers (if using wood skewers, soak in water at least 30 minutes first). Grill about 10 to 12 minutes, turning occasionally, or until meat is done.

Remove meat from grill; cover with aluminum foil while heating the pita loaves. Brush pita loaves with olive oil and grill until warm and just starting to spot.

Divide meat between pita loaves and top with red onion, tomatoes and tzatziki sauce.

Tzatziki Sauce
Source: Evangelos Nantsis

1 cucumber
16 ounces plain Greek yogurt
2 cloves garlic, minced, or to taste
Salt and pepper

Peel the cucumber and slice in half lengthwise. Scoop the seeds out of the cucumber and grate the cucumber. Place the grated cucumber in a colander and press out as much liquid as you can with your hands.

Add the cucumber to the yogurt along with the garlic, salt and pepper. Refrigerate until ready to serve.

Banoffee Pie
Michael and Kathleen Webb love all things English, including pub food like this pie. Note: Use caution in following the recipe's directions for making toffee.
Source: Michael Webb

Crust:
*1 package (16 ounces) chocolate wafers, graham crackers,
vanilla wafers or shortbread
6 tablespoons butter, melted*

Pie:
*1 pint whipping cream
1 teaspoon vanilla
3 cans (14 ounces each) sweetened condensed milk
3 bananas, sliced*

Toppings (optional):
Shaved chocolate bar, ground espresso beans, chopped walnuts or peanuts

For the crust, crush the cookies and mix with melted butter. Crushed walnuts, peanuts or almonds can also be added to the crust. Using a fork or fingers, press the cookie crumbs into a pie pan. Make sure that there are no holes. Chill.

For the whipped topping, chill a glass bowl and the whipping cream. After chilling, pour whipping cream into bowl and add 1 teaspoon vanilla. Whip until soft peaks form.

To make the toffee sauce, remove the labels from the cans of condensed milk and immerse the cans unopened in a pot of water. Boil the cans for 2 to 3 hours. The longer you boil it, the darker and thicker the toffee will be. Make sure that the cans are fully covered in water; otherwise, the cans may explode. You'll need to check the pot and top it off constantly during the boiling process.

Remove from the pot and let the toffee cool for 3 hours before opening.

When cool, use a spoon to spread toffee cream gently into the pie crust. It will be very thick.

Arrange the sliced bananas on top. Top with whipped cream. Top with shaved chocolate and crushed nuts if using. Chill and serve.

Note: To save time, use store-bought whipped cream and any kind of pie shell. Pie can also be made in ramekins for individual servings.

Jalapeño Poppers

Brian Rader fires up the grill in his driveway most weekends for the benefit of friends and family. While there's always a big hunk of meat slowly smoking, these appetizers cook within about 30 minutes.
Source: Brian Rader

Two dozen jalapeños (look for large, milder chiles)
1 block cream cheese
8 ounces shredded cheddar cheese, softened
1 package bacon

Cut jalapeños in half length wise; remove stems and seeds. In bowl, combine cheeses. Fill each half of a jalapeño with cheese mixture and stick halves back together. Cut bacon into pieces long enough to wrap once around the jalapeño. Secure with a toothpick. Cook over indirect 350-degree heat about 20 to 30 minutes or until bacon is done. (Poppers can also be made in an oven.)

Mama's Fried (and Baked) Chicken

Rossanne Thomson's mother made this chicken for nearly every Sunday family dinner. Rossanne has given the recipe out to dozens of friends who like the crispy chicken it produces.
Source: Rossanne Thomson

4 cups Crisco shortening
1 chicken, cut into 8 to 10 pieces
3 cups all-purpose flour
1 tablespoon Morton's Nature's Seasons blend
1 tablespoon minced dried garlic
1 tablespoon minced dried onion
1 tablespoon onion salt

Put shortening into electric skillet or heavy-bottomed pan. Heat oil to 350 degrees; do not allow to begin smoking.

Rinse chicken and set on paper towels; do not dry.

Mix all dry ingredients well. Roll chicken pieces in mixture until well coated. Place carefully in hot shortening without letting pieces touch each other. Cover pan.

Turn chicken after 5 to 7 minutes. Brown on each side until crisp and golden.

Line large broiler pan with foil; spray rack with cooking oil or rub with olive oil.

Lift browned chicken out of shortening and place on broiler pan rack. Place in preheated 350-degree oven about 30 to 40 minutes or until cooked through.

Pork Satay

Naam Pruitt was a popular guest teacher at Cooking at Bonnie's Place and the author of *Lemongrass & Limes*, a 2006 cookbook. This satay sauce is so good on rice you might want to double it.

Source: Naam Pruitt

1 can (14 ounces) coconut milk, divided use
2 teaspoons turmeric powder
1 teaspoon curry powder
1 tablespoon sugar
2 tablespoons soy sauce
2 pounds boneless pork loin chops or chicken breast, sliced into ⅛-inch-thick strips
Wooden skewers

Satay sauce:
¾ cup coconut milk
2 teaspoons red curry paste
¼ teaspoon coriander
2 tablespoons sugar
Salt, to taste
¼ cup salted peanuts, ground or chopped finely

Cooked jasmine rice

To make satay, combine 1 cup coconut milk, turmeric powder, curry powder, sugar and soy sauce together in a bowl. Add pork and marinate for 1 to 8 hours.

Soak skewers in water for 15 minutes to prevent burning. Remove pork from marinade, discarding the marinade. Thread pork onto skewers. Grill or broil about 3 inches from heat source about 3 to 4 minutes per side.

Serve with rice and satay sauce.

To make satay sauce, heat remaining ¾ cup coconut milk in a small saucepan over medium heat until bubbly. Add curry paste and coriander and whisk until blended. Add salt (if using) and sugar and stir to combine.

Add peanuts and cook for 5 minutes longer. Taste and adjust seasoning as desired.

Pad Thai
Source: Naam Pruitt

1 cup thinly sliced pork
1 teaspoon soy sauce, preferably light
½ (14-ounce) package rice noodles
¼ cup canola oil
2 large shallots, chopped
¼ cup extra-firm tofu, cubed
¼ cup sugar
¼ cup fish sauce
1 cup shrimp, shelled and deveined
3 eggs
3 cups bean sprouts (see note below)
½ cup regular or garlic chives
Garnishes: lime slices, chile powder, fish sauce, sugar and roasted peanuts

Marinate pork in soy sauce for 30 minutes to 1 hour. Soak rice noodles in warm water in a bowl for 20 minutes; drain.

Heat wok or large skillet over medium-high heat and add oil. Add shallots and fry until golden. Add pork and tofu and cook until pork is done.

Add noodles, sugar and fish sauce and cook until noodles are soft. Push noodles to the side of the wok and add shrimp. Cook until shrimp are light pink.

Push shrimp to the side with the noodles and add the eggs. Cook until the eggs are scrambled, stirring constantly.

Stir in bean sprouts and chives. Remove from heat.

Serve with separate bowls of lime slices, chile powder, fish sauce, sugar and roasted peanuts, which diners can add to their servings as desired.

Note: On the day you plan to use the bean sprouts, soak them in cold water and drain just before use.

*Ramped-Up Ramen

Yes, college students still eat ramen noodles, but in more creative ways than I did. One of my students in Butler Community College's culinary program showed me this recipe, which sounds strange but is something we now eat all the time.

1 package ramen noodles
1 slice American or Swiss cheese
Olive oil
1 egg
Salt and pepper
Sriracha

Adding cheese to instant ramen thickens the broth, while the fried egg provides protein and the sriracha lends heat.

Prepare ramen noodles as directed on package, using ½ cup less water than called for in directions. Pour noodles and their sauce into a bowl and top with slice of cheese. Meanwhile, heat oil in skillet over high heat. Fry egg until bottom is crispy but yolk is just barely set. Season with salt and pepper and top cheese with egg. Drizzle with sriracha and serve.

Cajun Pasta

Marc Hammann can often be found cooking where live music is playing. This recipe is equally tasty served over rice. Any leftover roux can be frozen or stored in the refrigerator.

Source: Marc Hammann

1 bell pepper, any color
1 yellow onion
2 stalks celery
2 green onions
1 pound cooked chicken, cut into bite-size pieces
1 cup diced ham
1 link Andouille sausage, sliced
1 quart chicken stock
1 can (16 ounces) diced tomatoes
1 teaspoon each dried thyme, oregano and garlic, plus salt, sage, onion powder, white pepper, cayenne pepper and black pepper to taste
Cooked pasta

For roux:
½ cup vegetable oil
½ cup flour

Chop all vegetables. Place in large pot with chicken, ham, sausage, chicken stock, tomatoes and seasonings. Add water, if necessary, to cover. Bring mixture to boil, then cover, reduce heat and simmer until vegetables are soft and sausage is cooked through.

To thicken, place 2 tablespoons of prepared roux (directions below) in a mixing bowl or pan, then stir in about 1 cup of hot liquid from pot; when combined, stir that mixture back into the pot. Repeat as necessary until desired thickness is reached. Taste, adjust seasonings and serve over cooked pasta or rice.

To make roux: Add oil to a cast-iron or other heavy skillet set over medium-low heat. Add flour and cook, stirring frequently, about 10 to 15 minutes or until mixture is a golden brown color with a nutty aroma. Do not let it burn.

*Fresh Egg Pasta
Nancy McMaster looks for new culinary experiences wherever she goes, so when she found herself sitting next to an Italian grandmother at a wedding, naturally she left with an authentic, easy-to-memorize formula for fresh pasta. Serve with a favorite sauce or simply toss with butter, fresh herbs and/or grated cheese.

1 cup flour
1 large egg, lightly beaten
½ eggshell of water (about 1 to 2 tablespoons)

Place flour in a bowl. Make a well in the center. Pour in egg and water. Stir together mixture, then use your hands to form it into a ball. Add flour if too wet, water if too dry. Wrap dough in plastic wrap and allow to rest for 20 minutes before rolling out and cutting into desired shape (or use a pasta maker to roll and cut pasta).

To prepare, add pasta to a big pot of boiling, salted water. Cook about 2 to 4 minutes, depending on thickness of pasta. For best results, allow pasta to dry at least 1 hour before cooking.

Popcorn Toppers

Andrea Cassell created these popcorn toppings to keep things interesting with a favorite snack. Cassell hosted a television segment, authored a Mediterranean cookbook (*Nahima's Hands*) and started a series of children's books based on a dog named Kibby while living here. She began writing a newspaper column in Georgia after moving there with her husband.

For all the recipes, place the specified amount of hot popcorn and remaining ingredients in a paper sack and shake well.

Spicy Popcorn:

8 cups hot popcorn
½ teaspoon sea salt
½ teaspoon chili powder
⅛ teaspoon garlic powder
⅛ teaspoon ground paprika
⅛ teaspoon ground cayenne pepper

Pepper Parmesan Popcorn:

8 cups hot popcorn
2 tablespoons extra-virgin olive oil
⅓ cup finely grated Parmesan cheese
½ teaspoon sea salt

Ranch Popcorn:

16 cups hot popcorn
1-ounce package ranch seasoning
2 tablespoons fresh chives
4 tablespoons melted butter
Sea salt, to taste

Frog Legs

Lest anyone think I turn my nose up at amphibians or the people who eat them, I include this recipe from Mike Dowell, who invited me to a frog leg fry in Linwood Park. Dowell patrolled the moonlit banks of ponds and rivers to catch his; you can order them online and sometimes find them in supermarkets.

Source: Mike Dowell

Frog legs
White wine
Spicy cornmeal-based breading mix, such as Andy's Red
Vegetable oil, for frying

If necessary, use sharp knife to separate legs. Marinate frog legs overnight in wine. When ready to cook, heat oil in skillet or deep fryer to 350 degrees. Remove legs from marinade, pat dry and coat in breading mix.

Cook about 3 to 5 minutes per side or until golden brown, turning once if using skillet.

Chapter 7

RESTAURANT REVEALS

If anything causes Carrie and me to split the apron, it probably will be a restaurant. As in her oft-repeated threat: "If you ever decide to open a restaurant, I will leave you."

Not that I have any desire to open a restaurant. But like any self-respecting food lover who fancies himself a cook, I have fantasized about what it would be like to have one.

It would be located on a beach, naturally, or down an alley in a big city, or in an old Tuscan villa. We're fantasizing, remember. Inside would be a clubby bar and a big, casual dining room. Out back would be a garden and a basketball hoop. Carrie would run the front of the house, putting names to faces, sending out amuse-bouches and champagne to favored guests. Those guests would be a mix of jet-setting celebrities and unfazed locals. Musicians between gigs would drop by to play for their supper. Supermodels would visit to bust their diets. I'd be in the kitchen with a staff of talented miscreants, driving them on to ever-higher levels of creativity and bailing them out of jail as necessary.

And the food? It'd be composed of the best ingredients we could find, prepared as simply as possible, with a chalkboard menu that changed from day to day and from lunch to dinner, depending on what local growers and purveyors had just brought to our back door. Red snapper caught a few hours before? Fire up the grill! A pail of fresh mozzarella? Let's do Italian!

The Food Network would come calling, but we'd shoo them away, telling them we couldn't possibly do any more business.

Clam chowder awaits a diner on the patio at Newport Gill. Wichitans love eating "out"—as in outdoors.

It's a fun fantasy but so at odds with what I know of the restaurant business that I'm not tempted to try it in real life. In the real world, most restaurants get most of their ingredients out of the back of the same large refrigerated trucks that stop at every other restaurant in town. From this, the owner must serve food that turns a profit after supplies, salaries, rent, utilities, taxes and other costs are deducted. Once a chef perfects a dish, he'd better like making it, because patrons will be outraged if it's taken off the menu. Slip a notch, quality wise, and there are a thousand other restaurants ready to take your place. Staff members quit, steal or just disappear. Customers complain, which would cause Carrie to cry and me to curse.

It's not all bad. I know restaurateurs who make great food, take good care of their customers and employees and make a fine living. Obviously, there's no shortage of people in this town willing to give the business a try. But it's no fantasy life.

Carrie can rest easy. I'll leave it to these professionals.

Luciano's Italian Restaurant: Pork Chops in Mushroom Cream Sauce

Luciano Mottola met his wife, Nancy, while she was teaching English in his native Italy. Together, they've induced a lot of Wichitans to drive fifteen miles south to Mulvane to eat simple, flavorful dishes like this one. Note the mushrooms are boiled in this recipe, a method that gives them a meaty taste and texture.

Makes 4 servings.

Source: Luciano Mottola

1 ½ pounds boneless pork chops or pork tenderloin
Salt and pepper, to taste
½ pound button or other favorite mushrooms, sliced
2 tablespoons butter
2 cups water
2 tablespoons olive oil
1 cup heavy cream

Season pork chops to taste with salt and pepper. If using tenderloin, cut into 4 equal-sized pieces. Make a horizontal slit along the side of each piece, almost but not all the way through, and open it the way you would a book.

In a small saucepan, place sliced mushrooms, butter and water. Heat to boiling and continue cooking until almost all the liquid has evaporated.

Meanwhile, heat 2 tablespoons olive oil in a sauté pan over medium heat. Add pork and cook, turning once, about 8 minutes or until done. (You might have to use two pans or do this in batches.) Remove pork from heat and cover to keep warm.

When almost all the liquid has evaporated from the mushrooms, add the cream and continue to boil about 5 minutes or until the cream thickens. Pour sauce over pork and serve.

Siena Tuscan Steakhouse:
Bistecca alla Fiorentina

Marshall Roth enjoyed a brief, flamboyant run as executive chef at Siena Tuscan Steakhouse in the Ambassador Hotel. He's still churning out glorious hunks of beef like this one, now as head chef at Butcher & Still in the Four Seasons Hotel Abu Dhabi, United Arab Emirates.
Makes 3–4 servings.
Source: Marshall Roth

Marshall Roth was game for just about anything while working as executive chef at Siena Tuscan Steakhouse, including grilling on a downtown rooftop so I could get a photograph of him with the Ambassador Hotel (where Siena is located) in the background.

3 pounds beef steak (T-bone, Porterhouse, rib-eye or KC Strip)
Salt and pepper
1 cup olive oil
2 tablespoons fresh oregano, chopped
2 tablespoons fresh parsley, chopped
1 tablespoon fresh thyme, chopped
5 cloves garlic, minced
1 shallot, minced
Zest and juice of 2 lemons
1 tablespoon salt, or to taste

Season steaks with salt and pepper. Grill over medium heat until desired doneness is reached, turning just once if possible (about 7 minutes total per inch for rare, 10 for medium rare or more for well done).

Meanwhile, in a bowl whisk together olive oil, herbs, garlic, shallot, lemon and salt.

Remove meat from fire and let rest, covered, about 5 minutes. Slice meat against the grain and place on a serving platter. Brush with herb–olive oil mixture and serve.

Note: The herb–olive oil recipe makes more than you'll need for this dish. Store the rest in the refrigerator and use within a few days. It's great on grilled chicken and fish.

Carrabba's: The Scotty Thompson

This super-simple and tasty starter was named for a customer of the original Carrabba's in Houston. Joe Parten took over the Wichita Carrabba's shortly after I published this recipe and continued to run the place more like a local restaurant than your typical chain eatery until his retirement.

Makes 2 servings.

Source: Carrabba's

½ pound goat cheese, cut into medallions
1 cup spaghetti sauce
Garlic bread
Fresh basil, for garnish (optional)

Place goat cheese medallions in an oven-proof serving dish. Pour spaghetti sauce around medallions and bake at 350 degrees until sauce is bubbly. Garnish with fresh basil, if desired, and serve with garlic bread.

Watermark Café: Great Expectations Sandwich

Years after the late Watermark Café chef Amy Kellogg adapted this recipe from a Junior League cookbook, it remains a favorite on the menu as the Great Expectations sandwich.

Makes 4 sandwiches.

Source: Watermark Café

Apricot Mayonnaise:

1 ½ cups mayonnaise
¼ cup apricot jam
1 ½ teaspoons curry powder

Sandwich:

8 slices focaccia
1 pound sliced smoked turkey
1 cup chopped walnuts, toasted
⅓ cup currants or raisins
1 cup salad greens

In a small bowl, combine mayonnaise, jam and curry powder. Whisk until well blended. Cover and chill until ready to use (up to 2 days).

Spread slices of focaccia with apricot mayo. Layer turkey, walnuts, raisins and salad greens between slices and serve.

*Restaurant 155: Seared Salmon

When the editors of *Cook's Illustrated* magazine asked me for a favorite local restaurant recipe, I immediately thought of this one from Tony Card of Restaurant 155, which was located in the old Lassen Hotel building. It was included in "Restaurant Favorites at Home" (*Cook's Illustrated*, 2003). Card served it with a tarragon aioli, but it also works well with fruit-based accompaniments such as the Mango-Cilantro Relish below.

Makes 2 servings.

Source: Tony Card

Chef Tony Card grew up in his dad Bill Reaves's jazz club and restaurant, Bill's Le Gourmet. *Courtesy of Tony Card.*

¼ cup olive oil
2 salmon fillets, about 8 ounces each
1 teaspoon kosher salt
½ teaspoon freshly cracked black pepper

Preheat oven to 500 degrees.

Heat oil over medium heat in oven-proof pan. Season salmon fillets with salt and pepper and sear in pan for 45 seconds to 1 minute on each side or until a crust forms. Remove pan with salmon from burner and place in oven for 7 to 8 minutes or until done.

Mango-Cilantro Relish

Natasha Gandhi-Rue, who owns The Kitchen in Old Town with her husband, Scott, shared this recipe when she was working at the Williams-Sonoma store in Bradley Fair.

Source: Natasha Gandhi-Rue

2 ripe mangoes, peeled and diced (one small bag of frozen mango chunks, defrosted, can be substituted)
½ red onion, finely sliced
2 tablespoons fresh cilantro, chopped
3 tablespoons lime juice
2 tablespoons orange juice
3 tablespoons extra-virgin olive oil
Kosher salt and freshly ground black pepper

Combine mangoes, onion, cilantro, juices and olive oil. Season with salt and pepper. Let sit for 30 minutes at room temperature. May be refrigerated for 1 day. Serve at room temperature.

Metro Grill: Cuban Sandwich
Michael Gonzalez first attracted attention cranking out gourmet hot dogs and sandwiches from a kiosk in Towne East Square. He eventually opened several Metro Grill locations around Wichita before legal and domestic woes put him out of business. His Cuban sandwich was as good as he claimed.
Source: Michael Gonzalez

Mojita:
2 cups sour orange juice (or combine 1 ⅓ cups orange juice with ⅔ cup lemon juice)
6 cloves garlic, minced
½ cup onion, chopped
½ cup green bell pepper, chopped
1 teaspoon salt
½ teaspoon pepper
Large pinch thyme
Large pinch tarragon

Roast Pork:
2–3 pounds pork loin roast

For Each Sandwich:
Hoagie bun

Roast pork
Swiss cheese, sliced
Ham, sliced
Pickle slices
Mustard
Reserved mojita sauce

Combine mojita ingredients. Set aside about ½ cup of the sauce for making sandwiches. Add pork loin to remaining mojita and refrigerate at least 4 hours, turning occasionally.

Transfer roast and marinade to a pan and cook, uncovered, at 250 degrees for 3 to 4 hours or until pork is done. Shred or slice pork thinly.

To make the Cuban: split hoagie bun in half lengthwise; lightly toast.

Layer pork, cheese, ham and pickles on lower bun. Top with mustard, mojita sauce and top half of bun and serve.

Pumphouse: Sloppy Joes

Seeing the Pumphouse today with its huge wraparound patio and big-screen TVs, it's hard to believe the Ross family's restaurant/sports bar/nightclub started out as a tiny diner inside an actual filling station. Judy Ross told me the recipe for these sweet-and-tangy Sloppy Joes came from a huge Labor Day picnic held for years in her hometown of Kiowa. It's still the Thursday special at the Pumphouse.

Source: Judy Ross

Although her sons now run the Pumphouse, Judy Ross still can occasionally be found in the kitchen of the Old Town favorite.

1 pound ground beef
Salt and pepper, to taste
⅓ cup ketchup
5 tablespoons mustard
5 tablespoons brown sugar
Hamburger buns
Garnish: Sliced red onion, shredded cheddar cheese

In a skillet, brown beef; drain well. Season to taste with salt and pepper. Stir in ketchup, mustard and brown sugar. Bring to a boil, reduce heat and simmer at least 20 minutes, or until mixture thickens slightly. Serve on a bun with red onion slices and shredded cheese.

Mama-Sans: Gyozas

Every time I ate at Mama-Sans, I left wondering why I didn't eat there more often (perhaps because it was open only three days a week). Akiko Miloni ran her Japanese restaurant on West 13th Street like she was cooking for friends in her home. She filled these dumplings just before frying, but they can also be prepared several hours in advance and kept refrigerated until fried. For a lower-fat version, cook the dumplings in a steamer.
Makes about 50 gyozas.
Source: Akiko Miloni

1 package gyoza wrappers (see note below) or wonton wrappers
½ pound ground beef
½ pound ground pork
2 tablespoons garlic, minced
1 egg, lightly beaten
Vegetable oil for frying

Defrost gyoza wrappers if frozen. To make filling, mix all ingredients except gyoza wrappers, egg and vegetable oil with your hands until well blended. Place about 1 teaspoon filling in the center of a wrapper. Dip finger into beaten egg and moisten edge of wrapper. Fold wrapper over and crimp edges to seal. Repeat with remaining ingredients.

Heat vegetable oil over medium-high heat. Lower gyozas into oil in batches and cook, turning once, about 2 to 3 minutes, or until golden brown. Serve hot with soy sauce, teriyaki sauce or spicy mustard.

Note: Gyoza wrappers can be found with frozen foods in Asian markets and some supermarkets. Wonton wrappers are often sold near bagged salads in supermarkets.

Mama-Sans: Yakisoba

This recipe uses inexpensive ramen noodles to make a stir-fry dish
rather than soup.
Makes 3–4 servings.
Source: Akiko Miloni

2 packages (3.6 ounces each) Japanese-style noodles, with seasoning packet,
preferably chow mein flavor
Vegetable oil
1 pound boneless, skinless chicken breasts, cut into ½-inch cubes
1 onion, thinly sliced
4 carrots, cut into matchsticks
⅓ head cabbage, shredded
Soy sauce or teriyaki sauce

Remove seasoning packet from noodle package and set aside. Boil
noodles in water until cooked, about 3 minutes; drain and set aside
(noodles can be prepared in advance and refrigerated).

Heat oil in wok or large skillet over medium-high heat. Add chicken
and stir-fry 1 to 2 minutes, until it is beginning to brown. Add vegetables
and stir-fry 3 to 4 minutes, until vegetables are crisp-tender and chicken
is cooked all the way through. Add noodles and contents of seasoning
packet to wok and stir-fry briefly, until heated through. Season to taste
with soy sauce or teriyaki sauce and serve.

Garozzo's Ristorante: Cavatelli Catania

I have a theory that certain restaurant locations are doomed. Take
Garozzo's, which opened with a bang, serving gargantuan portions of
Italian American favorites like this pasta dish. It lasted only a few years
(though its original Kansas City location remains open). Bella Donna and
the Lakeside Club later failed in the same spot.
Makes 4 servings.
Source: Michael Garozzo

1 pound cavatelli or other medium-size shell pasta
½ stick butter
1 cup red onion, diced

3 teaspoons garlic, chopped
1 cup fresh tomatoes, diced
2 cups fresh mushrooms, sliced
1 jar (26-ounce) Garozzo's or other pasta sauce
2 cups chicken stock
Salt and pepper, to taste
Freshly grated Romano cheese

Cook pasta al dente according to package directions. Drain and keep warm. Sauté onion and garlic in butter on medium-high. Add tomatoes and mushrooms and cook 2 to 3 minutes more. Add pasta sauce and blend for 1 minute. Add chicken stock and bring to a boil; season to taste with salt and pepper. Add cooked pasta, return to a boil and serve immediately, topped with grated Romano cheese.

Newport Grill: Clam Chowder

A seafood-focused menu and waterside setting have helped make Newport Grill one of the east side's most popular spots. The nightly show that resident ducks put on doesn't hurt, either.
Source: Newport Grill

2 cups clam juice
1 quart heavy cream
1 clove garlic, minced
2 slices bacon, diced
2 stalks celery, diced
1 half onion, diced
1 can (6.5 ounces) chopped clams
1 potato, peeled and diced
1 bay leaf
Thyme and freshly cracked black pepper, to taste

Place clam juice in saucepan and simmer until reduced by half. Add heavy cream and garlic to clam juice. Simmer until mixture is reduced by about one-third.

Meanwhile, fry bacon in skillet until crisp. Drain fat.

Turn heat under saucepan to low and add celery, bacon, onion, clams, potato, bay leaf and thyme. Cook until vegetables are tender. If thicker chowder is desired, thicken by adding a slurry of equal parts cornstarch and water to chowder while it cooks.

Old Mill Tasty Shop: Apple Bread Pudding

Old Mill Tasty Shop is a Wichita treasure. Where else can you get lunch and a genuine soda fountain ice cream sundae these days? When I first published this recipe from Old Mill matriarch Mary Wright, I mistakenly left out the apples. It's actually delicious with or without them.

Makes 12 to 15 servings.

Source: Mary Wright

8 cups whole wheat bread, cubed
2 cups sugar
8 eggs
3 cups half-and-half
1 tablespoon cinnamon
1 tablespoon vanilla
½ teaspoon nutmeg
2 cups apples, chopped

Brown Sugar Creme Fraiche:

½ cup brown sugar
1 cup heavy whipping cream
1 teaspoon vanilla
1 cup sour cream

Cube bread. In a large bowl, whisk together sugar and eggs until smooth. Add half-and-half, cinnamon, vanilla and nutmeg.

Add cubed bread and apples to mixture and blend well. Place in 13x9-inch pan. Cover with wax paper and seal tightly with aluminum foil.

Bake 1 hour at 350 degrees. Remove foil and paper. Bake 15 minutes more.

To make creme fraiche: let brown sugar sit in cream for 5 minutes. Pulse sugar and cream in food processor or blender until thick. Add vanilla and sour cream; pulse just to blend.

Jodee B's: Lasagna

Tulsa native Jodee Bradley moved to Wichita to help her family open a barbecue restaurant. She then worked in the aircraft industry and, after getting laid off, started her own catering operation. Bradley gives lasagna a twist by replacing ricotta cheese with sour cream.
Source: Jodee Bradley

Jodee Bradley has fed many of the city's movers and shakers thanks to connections she made in the aviation industry before starting her catering business.

12 lasagna noodles
1 medium onion, diced
4 tablespoons extra-virgin olive oil
2 pounds ground beef
2 jars spaghetti sauce
Salt and pepper, to taste
16 ounces sour cream
1 small package pepperoni slices
2 cups mild shredded cheddar cheese
2 cups shredded mozzarella cheese

Preheat oven to 375 degrees. Cook pasta according to package directions.

In a large skillet, sauté onion in olive oil until translucent, about 5 minutes. Add ground beef and brown. Add 1 ⅓ jars spaghetti sauce to beef, reserving the rest of the sauce, and bring to a boil. Add salt and pepper to taste.

Spray 9x13-inch pan with cooking spray. Spread half of remaining spaghetti sauce in dish. Layer 3 lasagna noodles over sauce and top with ⅓ beef mixture, ⅓ sour cream, 9 pepperoni slices, ¼ of the cheddar cheese and ¼ of the mozzarella cheese. Repeat with two more layers. Top with remaining 3 lasagna noodles. Pour remaining spaghetti sauce over top, cover with foil and bake for 30 minutes.

Remove foil; top with remaining mozzarella and cheddar cheese. Re-cover with foil. Bake another 15 to 30 minutes. Let lasagna rest 5 minutes before serving.

Roman-Style Strata Casserole

Peter Moretti, executive chef at the Wichita Marriott, is known for his expertise pairing food and wine. This recipe is one he makes for his family during the holidays.

Source: Peter Moretti

Butter for greasing 9x13x2-inch baking dish
8 slices multi-grain artisan bread
6 large eggs, lightly beaten
4 cups whole milk
16 ounces Fontina cheese, grated
Salt and pepper, to taste
1 tablespoon dried basil
1 tablespoon olive oil
1 red bell pepper, thinly sliced
4 ounces baby portabella mushrooms, sliced
1 handful baby spinach leaves
3 ounces hot capicola ham, cut into medium dice
½ cup parmesan cheese, grated
¼ cup Italian parsley, chopped

Butter baking pan.

Cut bread slices into cubes and place in baking dish.

Prepare savory custard: To lightly beaten eggs, add milk, grated Fontina, salt and pepper and dried basil. Stir together.

Pour savory custard mixture over bread cubes in baking dish.

Heat olive oil in a large skillet. Sauté red pepper, mushrooms, spinach leaves and capicola until vegetables are soft. Lightly stir into bread and custard mixture in baking pan. Sprinkle with parmesan cheese and parsley. Let sit at least 20 minutes or overnight in refrigerator.

Bake in 345-degree oven for 50 to 60 minutes.

*Sumo by Nambara: Kansas Roll (Maki)

Horio Miyashita, sushi chef at Sumo by Nambara, showed me how anybody can make sushi at home. Of course, an *itamae* such as Miyashita spends years perfecting his craft; creativity and sourcing of ingredients are why most of us leave it to the pros. To clear up a common

misconception: sushi does not mean raw fish. It means anything made with "sushi rice" (see directions below). The nori (sheets of dried seaweed), sushi mat and wasabi (Japanese horseradish) called for in this recipe are available in Asian markets and the Asian section of many supermarkets.
Source: Horio Miyashita

Sushi rice:
1 pound short-grain rice (2½ cups)
3 cups water for cooking rice, plus more for washing
7 tablespoons rice wine vinegar
2 tablespoons sugar
1 tablespoon salt

Filling:
Wasabi powder
Mayonnaise
Seared beef tenderloin, sliced thin
Avocado slices
Daikon sprouts (other microgreens such as alfalfa or radish sprouts can be used)

10 sheets of nori

To wash the rice: place the rice in the saucepan in which you'll cook it. Cover with at least an inch of water and swirl with your fingers until the water is cloudy. Pour off the water and repeat this process until the water is no longer cloudy.

To cook the rice: after pouring off the water used to wash the rice, add 3 cups water. Bring the water to a boil, stirring just enough to keep rice from sticking to the bottom, then cover and reduce heat; simmer about 15 to 20 minutes, or until water is absorbed and rice is tender.

When rice is cooked and still hot, spread into a 13x9-inch pan.

Combine vinegar, sugar and salt. Sprinkle rice with vinegar mixture and then fold rice with spatula or big spoon, trying not to crush the rice kernels.

In a small bowl, stir together ½ tablespoon wasabi powder and 1 teaspoon water until a paste is formed. Stir in mayonnaise.

To make the roll, place one sheet of nori on the mat, shiny side down. When the rice is cool enough to handle but still warm, spread about

⅔ cup of it on the sheet, not more than ⅛ inch thick, leaving about 1 inch at the top of the sheet uncovered. Place the tenderloin, avocado and sprouts in a strip no more than ¾ inch high and wide across the bottom end of the sheet. Drizzle with wasabi-mayo mixture. Using the mat, roll the nori around the filling, pulling the mat back as necessary to avoid getting it caught in the roll; gently squeeze the mat to shape the roll. Remove the mat and cut the roll into 6 pieces.

Sakura: Japanese Omelet

One of Wichita's first sushi restaurants, Sakura has always offered more than just that specialty, from its days at Harry and Webb to its current home in Delano. Good cooking runs in the Sakura family: chef-owner Trian Tran's brother, Jacky, went on to open his own place as well. Serve this omelet as a lunch or dinner entrée, with plenty of rice to sop up the delicious sauce.
Source: Sakura

Omelet:
2 eggs
¼ teaspoon chicken bouillon
¼ teaspoon sugar
⅛ teaspoon salt

Filling:
½ cup chicken, chopped
¼ cup bell pepper, chopped
¼ cup onion, chopped
1 teaspoon garlic, chopped
1 tablespoon soy sauce
½ tablespoon oyster sauce
Black pepper
1 teaspoon sesame oil
1 teaspoon Japanese rice wine or cooking wine

Sauce:
1 teaspoon garlic, chopped
⅓ cup teriyaki sauce

1 teaspoon cornstarch mixed with 1 teaspoon water
Minced green onions, for garnish

Lightly beat eggs together with chicken bouillon, sugar and salt.

Heat 1 tablespoon vegetable oil in nonstick or well-seasoned skillet set over medium-high heat. Add chicken, bell pepper, onion and garlic. Sauté until chicken is just cooked through. Stir in soy sauce, oyster sauce, pepper, sesame oil and rice wine. Remove to a plate.

Heat 1 tablespoon vegetable oil in skillet over medium heat and add eggs. Swirl until egg is thinly spread around skillet. Using a spatula, loosen edges as soon as egg is set.

Spread chicken mixture in center of egg and fold edges over and around it to form a square or rectangle. Remove omelet to a plate and keep warm.

To make sauce, heat ½ teaspoon oil in skillet set over high heat and sauté garlic about 30 seconds. Add teriyaki sauce, then cornstarch-water mixture. Cook, stirring, about 30 seconds or until thickened.

Pour sauce over omelet, garnish with minced green onion and serve.

Granite City Brewery: Blue Peppercorn Burger

Granite City's Minnesota-based owners pulled out of Wichita despite seeming to sell plenty of good craft beer and food like this burger. The chain was an early entrant in Wichita's microbrewery scene (although purists pointed out that its "mash" of fermented grain, the first step in brewing, was made elsewhere).

Source: Granite City Brewery

1 pound ground beef
2 teaspoons freshly cracked black pepper
⅓ cup chunky blue cheese dressing
2 slices cheddar cheese
2 large sesame buns, toasted
2 slices cooked bacon
Onion strings (see note)

Form beef into two patties. Sprinkle top and bottom of patties with pepper.

Broil or pan-fry burger until desired doneness is just about reached. Divide blue cheese dressing and cheddar cheese between burgers and continue cooking until cheese is melted (if pan-frying, cover the pan with a lid to help melt the cheese).

Place burgers on buns and top with bacon and onion strings.

To make onion strings: heat 1 inch of vegetable oil in a small saucepan over medium-high heat. Slice half a yellow onion thinly; dust slices in flour. Fry in oil until golden brown; place on paper towel to drain.

Sweet Basil: Strawberry Flambé

Any time you get to set food on fire—on purpose—it's bound to be a good time. This dessert was prepared tableside at Sweet Basil, Charli Singh's Italian spot on Woodlawn.
Source: Charlie Singh

Diners at Charli Singh's Sweet Basil enjoyed a flaming dessert prepared tableside. *Courtesy of Charli Singh.*

2 pats butter
2 heaping tablespoons brown sugar
Juice from ½ orange
2 cups sliced strawberries (can substitute other favorite berries)
1 shot Cognac
½ shot Grand Marnier
½ teaspoon ground cinnamon
4 cups ice cream
Whipped cream

Melt butter in a sauté pan. Add brown sugar and mix with butter over medium-low heat. Do not burn.

When sugar has caramelized, squeeze juice from orange half (wrap the orange in a napkin or paper towel before squeezing to catch seeds, or use purchased orange juice). Add sliced strawberries and cook for 1 minute.

Add liqueurs. Carefully ignite liqueur with match or lighter. Sprinkle ground cinnamon over flames (it will spark).

Pour sauce over ice cream and top with whipped cream.

Timberline Steakhouse: Baked Sweet Potatoes

Baked sweet potatoes might have been as popular as the namesake dish
at Timberline Steakhouse, the small chain that Scott Redler and the late
Bill Simon ran before starting Freddy's Frozen Custard & Steakburgers
with Bill's brother, Randy.
Source: Timberline Steakhouse

Medium sweet potatoes
Salted butter
Cinnamon-sugar

Preheat oven to 375 degrees. Scrub and dry sweet potatoes. Place on
a baking sheet and cook for 45 minutes to 1 hour or until knife inserted
into potato easily goes all the way through.

Remove from oven and serve with butter and a dash of cinnamon-
sugar.

Rock Island: Chicken Salad

As a Cohlmia married to a Farha, it's no wonder Chris Farha found
her way into the food business. Farha helped pioneer Old Town's food
scene back in the 1990s with her Rock Island restaurant. Farha, who
went on to become director of food service for Kapaun Mount Carmel
and Bishop Carroll high schools, still gets requests for this chicken salad
recipe featuring an unusual mixture of sweet and crunchy ingredients.
Source: Chris Farha

1 cup mayonnaise
3 ounces juice from pineapple can
1 teaspoon almond extract
1 teaspoon basil
1 teaspoon oregano
1 teaspoon tarragon
2½ pounds cooked chicken, diced
2 cups canned pineapple chunks, drained, liquid reserved
1½ cups celery, diced

1 cup carrots, shredded
1 cup water chestnuts, sliced

Mix mayonnaise, pineapple juice, almond extract and spices until well blended. Fold in other ingredients. Chill and serve on a bed of lettuce or stuffed in pita bread. Top with toasted almonds, if desired.

Hana Café: Spicy Soft Tofu Soup
Eunice Kim of Hana Café is an Old Town Square pioneer, not only moving her restaurant there but living there as well. Although Hana is known for sushi, Kim is from Korea, where this soup is popular.
Makes 1 large or 2 medium servings.
Source: Eunice Kim

1 teaspoon vegetable oil
2 tablespoons onion, chopped
2 tablespoons zucchini, chopped
½ tablespoon ground red pepper
3 cups seafood broth
½ teaspoon beef bouillon paste
1 teaspoon Korean chile paste, such as Gochujang
½ cup seafood mixture, such as shrimp and mussels
¾ package soft tofu
1 tablespoon scallions, chopped

Eunice Kim prepares soup in a traditional Korean stone bowl.

Heat oil in a saucepan over medium-high heat. Add onion and zucchini; cook 2 minutes or until onion softens. Stir in red pepper and cook 30 seconds, until fragrant.

Add broth, bouillon and chile paste. Bring liquid to boil. Add seafood mixture, reduce heat and simmer until cooked through. Add tofu to broth, breaking up with a large spoon. When all ingredients are heated through, transfer to warm bowl, garnish with scallion and serve.

Note: Chicken broth and chopped chicken can be substituted for the seafood and broth. Soft tofu and Korean chile paste can be found in Asian markets and some supermarkets.

A barista at Espresso to Go Go prepares the Italian dessert known as Affogato, made by dousing a scoop of vanilla ice cream with a shot of espresso. The contrast of hot, cold, sweet and bitter flavors is delicious.

Doo-Dah Diner: Hot Brown

Doo-Dah Diner gets a nationally televised shout-out just about any time an ESPN crew is in town to do a Shocker basketball game. This tasty twist on a Kentucky Hot Brown sandwich has been a Doo-Dah staff favorite for years.
Source: Patrick Shibley, Doo-Dah Diner

4 slices maple-pepper bacon, divided use
About 2 tablespoons butter
¼ cup onion, chopped
4 tablespoons flour
2 cups heavy cream
½ cup sliced brie (rind removed), brought to room temperature
Salt and pepper, to taste
2 slices good Italian bread
10 ounces honey roasted turkey
2 slices ripe tomato

To make sauce: cook bacon in medium heavy-bottomed saucepan until fat is rendered. Set 2 pieces of bacon aside. Dice remaining bacon and return to saucepan. Melt enough butter in pan so that there are about 4 tablespoons of butter and bacon fat combined in saucepan. Sauté onion in pan until soft. Stir in flour and cook, stirring, about 30 seconds or until roux is formed. Slowly whisk in heavy cream, stirring frequently, and cook until mixture thickens. Add brie to sauce and remove from heat. When sauce has cooled somewhat, place it in a blender (or use an immersion blender) and blend until smooth. Return to saucepan. Season to taste with salt and pepper.

To make Hot Brown, preheat oven broiler. Place bread slices on oven-proof tray or serving dish. Layer turkey, tomato slices, sauce and bacon slices on bread. Broil until sauce begins to brown in spots, remove from oven and serve.

Mr. Steak: Beef Kabobs

Sid Bruner had been out of the restaurant business for several years by the time I reached Wichita, but he was still "Mr. Steak" to many who'd eaten in his place by that name on 21ˢᵗ Street. Although Mr. Steak was part of a nationwide chain, Bruner came up with this kabob recipe on his own. When it came to standard steak preparation, Bruner gave this sound advice: 1.) Buy meat in big, multipound chunks that you can cut into individual steaks of whatever thickness you prefer 2.) Age steak for a week or two in the refrigerator to get that slightly "high" or tangy taste that costs extra in high-end steakhouses 3.) Keep the seasoning simple and 4.) Most importantly, don't overcook the meat!

Source: Sid Bruner

½ cup pickle relish
1 cup Thousand Island salad dressing
1 cup vegetable oil
1 teaspoon garlic powder
2 pounds top sirloin, cut into 1-inch chunks
Onions, green pepper, cherry tomatoes and mushrooms

Mix relish, salad dressing, oil and garlic powder to make marinade. Place sirloin in marinade and refrigerate at least 4 hours or overnight.

Cut onions and green pepper into 1-inch pieces. Thread on skewers with pieces of sirloin, tomatoes and mushrooms.

Grill over medium heat, turning several times, until done, about 10 to 15 minutes.

GreenAcres: Smoothies

GreenAcres has been flying the natural foods banner in Wichita longer than any other business. From its flagship store in Bradley Fair, the business expanded to four locations in Wichita, two in Oklahoma and one in Missouri without ever losing the friendly vibe of a place that really believes its mission is to help customers.

Source: GreenAcres

Berry Blitz:
2 ounces strawberries
2 ounces bananas

Matt Murray tends to the organic produce in GreenAcres' east Wichita store.

2 ounces raspberries
2 ounces blueberries
6 ounces apple juice

Nutty Nana:
1 cup soy or almond milk
2 ounces bananas
1 tablespoon almond butter
2 whole dates with pits removed

Place ingredients in blender and liquefy enough to achieve desired thickness.

Mama Love's: Baked Macaroni and Cheese

The Love family is known for its accomplishments in music, sports and not least of all food thanks to Mama Love's, a soul food restaurant that enjoyed a four-year run in Old Town. Niki Love—the granddaughter of Ahnawake "Mama" Love—carried that legacy forward as a caterer and then culinary instructor at Butler Community College and the Boys and Girls Club in north Wichita. I got this recipe from her not long after her students at the latter had baked cookies for President George W. Bush.

Source: Niki Love

1 package (12 ounces) elbow macaroni

Sauce:
2 cups milk
1 stick butter
1 block processed cheese, such as Velveeta
1 cup shredded cheddar cheese
2 teaspoons onion powder
2 teaspoons garlic powder
1 teaspoon salt
1 teaspoon black pepper

Topping:
2 cups shredded Colby and Monterey Jack blend
½ cup fine bread crumbs

Cook pasta according to package directions; drain.

Meanwhile, in saucepan, heat together milk, butter, processed cheese, cheddar cheese, onion powder, garlic powder, salt and pepper until mixture is smooth. Remove from heat.

Stir together cooked pasta and sauce. Pour mixture into 13x9-inch baking pan.

Top with Colby/Monterey Jack cheese blend and bread crumbs. Bake in a 400-degree oven for 30 to 40 minutes or until top is golden brown and bubbly.

Wichita Country Club: White Chocolate Cheesecake

Damien Lehman possessed a skill that separated him from most Wichita chefs: he was an expert ice carver. Since ice carving requires a chainsaw, we'll stick with one of his other specialties: chocolate. This recipe makes 1 large or 2 small cheesecakes.
Source: Damien Lehman

Crust:
3 cups chocolate graham crackers, crushed finely
1 ½ sticks butter, melted
½ cup sugar

Pie filling:
2½ pounds cream cheese
2 cups sugar
¼ cup flour
2 teaspoons vanilla extract
5 whole eggs
2 egg yolks
9 ounces white chocolate, chopped into raisin-size pieces
¼ cup half-and-half

Optional glaze:
¼ cup corn syrup
3 tablespoons water
2 tablespoons butter
½ pound chocolate chips

To make crust, mix graham cracker crumbs, melted butter and sugar. Press into pie pan(s) or springform pan(s). Place in freezer for 15 minutes.

Cream the cheese. Add sugar, flour and vanilla. On low speed, beat well using a mixing paddle. Add eggs and yolks a little at a time. Scrape sides and resume beating.

Add chocolate and half-and-half. Pour filling into crust. Bake 1 hour at 300 degrees, or until outer edge is set and center is slightly jiggly (the outer edge may brown slightly and crack before the center is done). Cool completely before refrigerating.

To make glaze: bring corn syrup, water and butter to a boil over medium heat, stirring often. Remove from heat and immediately add chocolate. Stir until smooth in consistency. Drizzle over cheesecake and serve.

Angelo's: Orange Roughy with Scallions, Artichoke Hearts and Almonds

Angelo and Anna Fasciano started selling cooked pizzas out of their home in Derby in 1958, opening their first restaurant in Wichita the next year. The restaurant's loaded pizzas and baked pasta dishes are prime examples of what my clever former *Eagle* colleague Denise Neil calls "Wichitalian" food, but this lighter fish recipe is tasty, too.
Makes 2 servings.
Source: Angelo's

2 orange roughy filets, about 8 ounces each
1 tablespoon Worcestershire sauce
⅛ cup white wine
1 teaspoon lemon juice
⅛ cup seasoned bread crumbs
½ stick butter, divided use
Paprika

Topping:

2 artichoke hearts, halved
¼ cup scallions, chopped
⅛ cup almonds, toasted and slivered

Wichitans rejoiced when Angelo's, one of the city's oldest restaurants, reopened after a ten-year hiatus. *Courtesy of Jack Fasciano.*

Preheat oven to 500 degrees.

Lightly oil a baking dish big enough to hold two filets. Place filets in dish. If one end is especially thin, fold about an inch of it under the rest of the filet so that the fish will cook evenly.

Sprinkle the Worcestershire sauce, wine and lemon juice evenly over the filets. Sprinkle with bread crumbs. Melt half the butter and pour it over the filets. Sprinkle with paprika for color. If the bottom of the pan is not completely covered with liquid, add a bit of water. Bake in oven about 8 to 10 minutes, or until fish flakes easily when pressed with your finger or a fork; don't overcook or fish will be dry.

Meanwhile, melt the remaining butter in a pan and sauté the artichoke hearts, scallions and almonds until heated through. Garnish the baked filets with the artichokes, scallions and almonds and serve.

Café Elena: Shashlyk (Russian Shish Kabobs)

Photographer Fernando Salazar and I still talk about the time we went on a picnic with Elena Chuksina, then owner of Café Elena, and some of her Russian friends at Bartlett Arboretum in Belle Plaine. It was set up as a photo shoot but soon turned into a party, as we learned that a Russian picnic requires plenty of singing and vodka. The food, very similar to that served in her restaurant, was simple and good.

Side note: To properly enjoy vodka, serve it straight, chased with a pickled cherry tomato and loud "hoo-ah," similar to the exclamation of U.S. Marines.

Source: Elena Chuksina

3–4 pounds chicken pieces
1 jar mayonnaise
1 tablespoon vinegar
2 large onions, one sliced and one cut into eighths
Salt, pepper and garlic powder, to taste
2 bell peppers, chopped

Combine chicken, mayonnaise, vinegar, sliced onion and seasonings in a large bowl or resealable plastic bag. Refrigerate overnight.

When ready to cook, heat grill to medium-high. Alternate chicken pieces on skewers with onion and bell pepper pieces.

Grill until chicken is cooked through.

Russian Potato Salad
Source: Elena Chuksina

3 large baking potatoes
4 eggs
1 large carrot, sliced
1 cucumber, chopped
1 can peas, drained
1 bunch green onions, chopped
2 cups mayonnaise
Salt and pepper

Cook potatoes and eggs until done. When cool enough to handle, peel and chop.

Combine in a large bowl with vegetables. Toss with mayonnaise, season to taste with salt and pepper and serve.

Il Primo Espresso Café: Scones

Like craft beer, good coffee has established itself in Wichita and shows no indication of going away. Il Primo in Normandie Center keeps its loyal clientele coming back in part by serving food that just tastes better with a hot cup of coffee—like these buttery, crumbly scones. Former owner Debbie Howell said the key to these scones is not to use an electric mixer. To get the scones' proper crumbly texture, she said, "You gotta do it by hand."

Source: Il Primo Espresso

1 cup sugar
6 cups flour
1 ½ tablespoons baking powder
½ teaspoon salt
2 sticks butter
4 ounces cream cheese
1 ½ cups buttermilk
1 cup dried fruit, roughly chopped (see note below)

Mix all dry ingredients together, then cut in butter and cream cheese. Add buttermilk and dried fruit. Form into scones and bake at 350 degrees for 25 minutes.

Note: Il Primo often uses dried cherries or raspberries for its scone filling. For Valentine's Day, try dried strawberries and white chocolate chips.

Chester's Chophouse: Bourbon Black Bottom Pie

Bobby Lane put this decadent dessert on the menu when he was chef-owner at Chester's. He describes it as a basic pecan pie that a southern grandmother added chocolate and bourbon to.

Makes 2 pies.
Source: Bobby Lane

Pie crust:
3 cups all-purpose flour
½ tablespoon sugar
½ teaspoon salt

½ pound (two sticks) softened butter
6 tablespoons and 1 teaspoon milk

Pie filling:
6 eggs
2 cups sugar
2 cups dark corn syrup
¼ pound (1 stick) butter, melted and cooled to room temperature
½ cup bourbon
½ tablespoon vanilla
2 cups bittersweet chocolate (chips or chunks), chopped
2 cups white chocolate (chips or chunks), chopped
2 cups pecans, chopped

To make the pie crust: mix flour, sugar and salt. Add butter and milk alternately (adding more milk if needed). Form dough into two balls and chill 2 hours before rolling out and filling pie pans.

To make the filling: whisk together eggs, sugar, corn syrup, melted butter, bourbon and vanilla. Fold in chocolates and pecans. Fill pie shells and bake on bottom rack at 325 degrees for 45 minutes or until filling is set.

Store pie in the refrigerator, but bring back to room temperature before serving.

Redrock Canyon Grill: Rotisserie Chicken

For a brief period, I wanted to *be* Brad Johnson, corporate chef for the company that owns Red Canyon Grill. Who wouldn't want to get paid to create delicious recipes like this but not have to toil away in a restaurant kitchen? (Eventually, I realized I'd actually need Johnson's culinary credentials and talent to get that kind of job.) Redrock makes its signature chicken on a rotisserie, but the rub also works great on a chicken cooked by other methods.
Source: Brad Johnson

1 whole chicken, about 4 pounds
1 teaspoon kosher salt
1 teaspoon black pepper, preferably freshly cracked

1 teaspoon dried thyme
1 teaspoon dried rosemary
2 teaspoons minced garlic
½ teaspoon dried marjoram
½ teaspoon paprika
Pinch cayenne

Remove giblets from chicken cavity and cut off wing tips; reserve for other use. Wash chicken inside and out.

In a small bowl, combine salt, pepper, thyme, rosemary, garlic, marjoram, paprika and cayenne. Rub about 1 tablespoon of mixture inside cavity. Loosen skin over breast with your fingers and work about 1 teaspoon of mixture between the skin and breast. Rub remaining mixture over outside of skin.

Truss legs with twine or kitchen ties. Place on rotisserie according to manufacturer's directions and cook about 1 hour, or until temperature in thigh measures 165 degrees.

❖ ❖ ❖

Reverie Coffee Roasters:
Rye Chocolate Chip Cookies

Stephanie Hand's career has been fun to watch. She was barely a teenager when she started baking at the old Riverside Perk, now R Coffeehouse. She worked for Melad Stephan at Uptown Bistro and Oeno Wine Bar before winning a scholarship to the Cooking Institute of America in Hyde Park, New York. After graduating and working as a private chef on the East Coast, including a stint on a yacht, Hand returned home to create the inventive original food menu at Reverie's café. More recently, she's headed back east to work at The Rhu, a café and bakery in Asheville, North Carolina.
Source: Stephanie Hand

Stephanie Hand has taken her cooking skills to the East Coast and back.

3 cups dark chocolate chunks
4 cups all-purpose flour
1 cup rye flour

1 teaspoon baking soda
3 teaspoons kosher salt
1 ½ cups unsalted butter, softened
1 ½ cups brown sugar
1 ½ cups granulated sugar
2 eggs
1 tablespoon vanilla
2 teaspoons Maldon sea salt (smoked Maldon can be used)

Chop 2 cups chocolate into pea-sized pieces and remaining 1 cup into larger chunks. Combine flours, baking soda and kosher salt in separate bowl. Cream together softened butter and sugars until light and fluffy, scraping sides of bowl. Add eggs and vanilla to creamed butter mixture until fluffy. On low speed, add flour mixture in 3 parts. Fold in chopped chocolate, then chunks.

Portion into 4-ounce balls and flatten to ¾ inch thick on parchment-lined baking sheets. Sprinkle dough with Maldon salt generously (some will fall off during baking and transport). Bake at 375 degrees for 12 to 15 minutes. Cookies should still look raw in center. They will finish cooking as they cool. Let cool on baking sheet for 10 minutes before removing.

Pig In Pig Out BBQ: Basic Brisket Rub

The late Ron Cochran started Pig In Pig Out in a tiny former Tastee Freeze on South Hydraulic. His son, Derek, moved it to a bigger space on 13th Street and expanded the menu. The jillion or so cookoff medals and ribbons on the walls attest to the Cochrans' skill with a smoker and rubs like this.
Source: Ron Cochran

The right rub is the first step in producing great barbecue. Hours of low, slow cooking follow. *Photo by Brian Rader.*

¼ cup coarse ground pepper
¼ cup seasoned salt
2 tablespoons onion salt
2 tablespoons garlic salt

1 tablespoon ground mustard
2 tablespoons paprika
2 tablespoons chili powder

Combine ingredients. Use about 1 tablespoon seasoning per pound of brisket.

Larkspur: Veal Piccata
Larkspur has anchored the Douglas Avenue entrance to Old Town for decades, keeping a loyal clientele happy with a cozy patio, live music and time-tested favorites like this.
Makes 1 serving.
Source: Ty Issa

6 ounces veal cutlets (a chicken cutlet, pounded thin, can be substituted)
Flour, for dredging
Salt and pepper
Olive oil
⅛ teaspoon garlic, minced
1 tablespoon capers
1 lemon half
Dry white wine, such as sauvignon blanc
Fresh chopped parsley
Chopped pimiento

Dust veal lightly with flour and season to taste with salt and pepper.

Heat olive oil until hot in a sauté pan. Place veal in pan and cook about 1 minute per side or until lightly browned.

Add the garlic, then the capers. Squeeze lemon juice into pan around veal, then add wine. Cook about 30 more seconds, then place veal on plate, pour over the pan juices and garnish with parsley and pimiento.

Seafood Shoppe: Grilled Fish Tacos

The delicate flesh of fish presents some challenges when grilled, but the payoff is a filling that goes perfectly with the usual taco toppings. The owners of the Seafood Shoppe suggest you: 1.) Choose fish and seafood that's relatively firm, such as halibut, salmon or shrimp 2.) Oil fish before grilling 3.) Use a combination of tongs and spatula to turn fish or buy a grill basket and 4.) Avoid overcooking; fish is done when it easily flakes with your fingers or a fork.

Source: Seafood Shoppe

½ cup canola oil
2 teaspoons ground cumin
2 teaspoons chili powder
2 pounds halibut fillets, or other flavorful white fish
such as sea bass or red snapper
8 corn or flour tortillas
1 red bell pepper, halved and seeded
1 yellow bell pepper, halved and seeded
1 red onion or 1 bunch green, cut in slices
Avocado Salsa (see recipe below), sour cream, lime wedges and
cilantro sprigs for garnish

Clean grill and prepare for medium to medium-high heat. In a small bowl, combine the oil, cumin and chili powder. Place fish in a small dish and pour marinade over fish. Marinate about 30 minutes.

Wrap tortillas in foil and place on edge of grill and let them heat about 10 minutes per side.

Place the peppers, onion slices and fish fillets on the grill rack. Cook the onions and peppers until softened and browned, about 4 to 5 minutes. Cook the fish fillets, turning once, until browned and opaque throughout, 3 to 4 minutes per side. Transfer fish, onions and peppers to a plate and cut fish into strips.

Place 2 tortillas on each of 4 plates. Divide the peppers, onions and fish among the tortillas, top with avocado salsa and sour cream. Garnish with cilantro and lime wedges.

Avocado Salsa

2 tomatoes, diced
⅓ cup red onion, diced

⅓ cup fresh cilantro, chopped
¼ to ½ fresh jalapeño, seeded and minced
1 clove garlic, minced or pressed
1–2 tablespoons fresh lime juice
2 Haas avocados, diced
Salt and pepper, to taste

Combine ingredients in a bowl and let sit at room temperature about 30 minutes to let flavors marry. This can be made in advance, but wait to add the avocado until an hour or so before you serve.

Note: 1 cup chopped pineapple or mango can be substituted for the avocado.

*Bella Luna: Cheese Castle

Once a person experiences the cheese displays Matteo Taha puts together at Bella Luna, it is impossible to go back to the usual cheese trays featuring rubbery chunks of cheddar and pepper jack. The exact makeup might depend on who is ordering, but Taha has a knack of pairing and contrasting cheeses—rich and creamy, hard and soft, mild and ripe.

Source: Matteo Taha

Choose at least three of the following:
Feta: Crumbly, salty
Havarti: Mild, often flavored with dill
Boursin: Flavored cream cheese
Brie: Soft, mellow
Smoked cheddar: Semi-hard with hint of smoke
Fresh mozzarella: Soft, milky
Roquefort: Sharp blue cheese

Arrange big hunks of cheese on a serving platter with cheese knives. Surround with pita chips, olives, gherkins, tomatoes and Lebanese cucumbers; drizzle platter lightly with a balsamic vinaigrette.

Louis Café: Panzanella (Italian Bread Salad)

This dish originated in Italy's Tuscany region, probably as a way to make sure old bread didn't go to waste. It can't taste better anywhere than it does with freshly grown Kansas tomatoes and basil. The recipe comes from Louis Foreman of the Louis Café in Rose Hill.

Source: Louis Foreman

Louis Foreman's small-town café is known for burgers, southern food and nightly specials.

½ loaf Italian or French bread
½ cup extra-virgin olive oil
¼ cup red wine vinegar
Salt and pepper
4 medium to large ripe tomatoes, chopped
1 handful fresh basil leaves, minced

Cut bread into 1-inch cubes and place uncovered in bowl for several hours or until slightly stale. Make vinaigrette by whisking or shaking together olive oil, red wine vinegar, salt and pepper. Just before serving, add tomatoes and basil to bowl, toss with vinaigrette and serve.

Thai Tradition: Volcano Soup

I once watched my wife break into a sweat eating a dish at Thai Tradition, Wichita's oldest full-service Thai restaurant. We'd ordered the dish "hot" (about halfway between the "mild" and "chef's hot" options). This soup is not particularly spicy, unless you spoon in additional chile paste. You'll need to visit an Asian market to find lemongrass, galangal root and lime leaves. And you'll be glad you did. (Note: The lemongrass, galangal root and leaves are there only for seasoning, not eating.)

Source: Kay Pomatmat

2¼ cups chicken broth
3–4 pieces sliced lemongrass, about ½ stalk
2 pieces dried galangal root
2 fresh lime leaves, halved
½ tomato, cut into quarters

¼ yellow onion, diced
1–2 tablespoons fresh squeezed lime juice
1 tablespoon fish sauce or ½ teaspoon salt
1 tablespoon sweet chile paste (Thai Tradition uses Pantai Norasingh brand)
3–4 peeled, deveined shrimp (31–35 per pound size)
2 scallops
2 New Zealand green mussels
4 sliced (thin) calamari (squid) tubes (optional)
3 pieces imitation crab flakes
3–4 mushrooms, sliced
1 tablespoon freshly chopped cilantro

Place broth in pot and bring to a simmer; add lemongrass, galangal root, lime leaves, tomato, onion, lime juice, fish sauce and chile paste.

Bring the liquid to a low boil, add seafood and cook 1 to 2 minutes. Add fresh mushrooms and turn off the heat.

Place soup in a bowl, top with cilantro and serve.

DeFazio's: Pasta Fagioli

Fagioli—beans—are an underrated part of Italian cuisine, but they're front and center in this hearty soup from one of Wichita's favorite Italian restaurants, which unexpectedly closed in 2021. Owner Pete DeFazio said the recipe dates back at least as far as his grandmother.
Makes 8 servings.
Source: Pete DeFazio

¼ cup prosciutto or pancetta, diced
½ medium onion, diced
1 rib celery, diced
1 carrot, diced
2 tablespoons olive oil
1 tablespoon garlic, minced
Pinch crushed red pepper
6 cups beef broth
½ cup marinara sauce or tomato sauce
5 cups cooked cannellini beans (2 15-ounce cans, drained and rinsed)

Salt and freshly ground black pepper
1 ½ cups dry ditalini pasta (can substitute ziti or elbow macaroni)
Parmigiano-reggiano cheese
Pepperoncini

Sauté prosciutto, onion, celery and carrot in olive oil until softened, about 5 minutes. Add garlic and red pepper; sauté an additional 5 minutes.

Add beef stock and marinara sauce and bring to a simmer. Add beans and bring to a slow boil. Season with salt and pepper to taste.

Add pasta and cook for 8 minutes, or until pasta is al dente. Remove from heat and let rest 10 minutes before serving.

Garnish each serving with cheese and pepperoncini.

Bel Ami: Filet Henry IV

Nabil Bacha whipped out this classic of French cuisine not long after opening Bel Ami, a downtown favorite of people attending events at Century II and Intrust Bank Arena. Bacha makes his bearnaise sauce from scratch. This recipe uses a convenient dry mix, which more than gets the job done when partnered with a red wine glaze, crab meat, artichoke bottoms and beef tenderloin.
Source: Nabil Bacha

1 package (0.9 ounce) bearnaise sauce mix (such as Knorr's)
4 beef tenderloin filets (6 ounces each)
Salt and pepper
5 tablespoons butter, divided use
1 cup red wine
4 canned artichoke bottoms
4 tablespoons crabmeat

Prepare bearnaise sauce according to package directions. Cover and refrigerate. Reheat shortly before preparing steaks.

Season filets with salt and pepper. In heavy, large skillet, melt 4 tablespoons butter over medium heat and cook steaks until done, about 3 to 4 minutes on each side. Remove filets to plate and cover to keep warm.

Pour red wine into same skillet and boil rapidly until reduced by half, scraping pan with spatula to free any meat particles.

Meanwhile, in separate pan, sauté artichoke bottoms in remainder of butter for a minute or two.

To assemble, place one artichoke bottom on each filet, fill with a tablespoon of crabmeat and top with bearnaise sauce and then with the red wine glaze.

Cargill Innovation Center: Thanksgiving Turkey

With its huge meat and poultry business headquartered in Wichita, it's not surprising that Cargill's downtown Innovation Center should be a prime source of expertise on cooking turkey. Senior research chef Janet Bourbon said that in her opinion, a simple recipe using a smaller bird and lower cooking temperature yields best results. If you're feeding a bigger crowd, consider cooking two turkeys. The "spatchcocked" turkey variation below allows a turkey to be cooked at higher heat in about half the usual time.

1 turkey, 12 to 15 pounds, thawed
Onion, quartered
Lemon, halved
Several sprigs fresh thyme
Kosher salt and freshly cracked black pepper
Melted butter

Preheat oven to 300 degrees. Rinse turkey and pat dry, removing giblets from cavity if present. Place turkey in roasting pan; fill cavity with onion, lemon and thyme. Sprinkle turkey with salt and pepper. Roast about 18 to 22 minutes per pound, basting with melted butter every 20 minutes, or until internal temperature in innermost part of thigh reaches 165 degrees (Bourbon strongly recommends using a meat thermometer to eliminate guesswork).

Spatchcocked variation: To spatchcock a turkey, cut away its backbone with kitchen scissors or shears. Then press or splay the bird out flat on a baking rack. Preheat the oven to 450 degrees. The flatter shape allows the turkey to cook faster and more evenly, with the dark thigh meat getting done before the white breast meat dries out. The higher cooking temperature imparts a crispy skin and deeply roasted color. A 15-pound turkey takes about 1½ hours.

Green Bean Salad
Serve your Thanksgiving turkey with this make-ahead side dish,
also from Cargill chef Janet Bourbon.
Source: Janet Bourbon

2 pounds green beans, trimmed
6 tablespoons olive oil
2 tablespoons red wine vinegar
2 teaspoons Dijon mustard
1 garlic clove, minced
Salt and pepper, to taste

Cook beans in plenty of boiling salted water until just short of crisp-tender (they will continue cooking after being drained). While the beans cook, whisk together remaining ingredients. Toss cooked beans into the dressing while still hot. Refrigerate beans until ready to serve.

*Smashed Potatoes
Another Cargill chef, Stephen Giunta, used to cook in the White House.
His take on mashed potatoes left one visitor to the Innovation Center
asking, "Who needs turkey?"
Source: Stephen Giunta

2 pounds Yukon Gold potatoes
1 tablespoon salt
6 cloves garlic, peeled
1 stick butter, melted
2 cups half-and-half
Salt and pepper, to taste

Wash potatoes well but do not peel; cut into quarters. Place potatoes, salt and garlic in pot and cover with water. Bring to a boil, then reduce heat and simmer until potatoes are tender.

Drain potatoes and mash with garlic, adding butter and half-and-half as you proceed. Season to taste with salt and pepper.

Marchello's: Capellini de Angelo

What's an Iranian couple doing running an Italian restaurant in a strip center in south Wichita? As the song goes, "Ain't that America?" Mikaeil and Shirin Afsharpour, who opened Marchello's in 1996, specialize in old-school Italian American dishes like this.

Source: Mikaeil Afsharpour

2 pounds boneless chicken breasts
1 cup Italian salad dressing
½ stick butter
4 tablespoons flour
1 quart heavy cream
½ cup grated Parmesan cheese, divided use
¼ teaspoon garlic, minced
¼ teaspoon Italian seasoning
Salt and pepper, to taste
1 egg yolk, slightly beaten
1 pound capellini or angel hair pasta
½ pound cooked, peeled shrimp
8 ounces broccoli, steamed
1 cup shredded mozzarella cheese

Marinate chicken breast in Italian dressing at least 1 hour or overnight. Remove chicken from marinade and grill or sauté until done. Slice into ¼-inch-thick strips and set aside.

Melt butter in a saucepan. Add flour and cook about 3 minutes, until mixture is bubbly. Slowly whisk in cream. Continue cooking over medium heat about 15 minutes, stirring often, until sauce thickens and is slightly reduced.

Remove sauce from heat. Add 1 tablespoon Parmesan cheese, garlic, Italian seasoning and salt and pepper to taste. When sauce has cooled slightly, stir in egg yolk.

Cook capellini or angel hair pasta according to package directions; drain.

When ready to serve, preheat oven to 350 degrees. Wet the bottom of oven-proof serving dishes with the alfredo sauce. Divide pasta between dishes. Layer with chicken, shrimp and broccoli over pasta. Pour remaining sauce over the top, then sprinkle with mozzarella and remaining Parmesan.

Bake about 15 minutes or until heated through and bubbly.

This recipe makes 6 very large, rich servings, or 8 to 10 moderate servings. It can also be made in a 13x9-inch casserole.

Chef Cole's Sweet Potato Pie
Greg Cole started the Little Bits cookie company and also taught in Butler Community College's culinary arts program.
Makes 2 pies.

Crust:
1 ¼ cups flour
1 tablespoon sugar
½ teaspoon salt
4 tablespoons butter, chilled
4 tablespoons shortening, chilled
3 tablespoons water or vodka, ice cold

Filling:
2 large baked sweet potatoes, mashed
1 stick butter, melted
½ can evaporated milk
2 eggs
1 ½ cups sugar
1 tablespoon cinnamon
1 tablespoon nutmeg
1 tablespoon vanilla

For crust: in a large bowl combine flour, sugar and salt. Using two forks or two knives, work the butter and shortening into the flour mixture until it looks like cornmeal with a few pea-size chunks in it and some chunks of dough are starting to hold together. Quickly stir in water or vodka until a dough forms (you may need to add another tablespoon of water or vodka if the air is very dry). Keep stirring the mixture until a ball of dough forms. Once there is a ball of dough with some cornmeal-looking bits on the bottom, knead the dough lightly in the

Greg Cole is interviewed by Beth Bower for her PBS Kansas documentary and cookbook *The Pie Way... Kansas Style.*

bowl to bring together. Flatten into disc and wrap in plastic wrap and chill for 30 minutes. Remove from the refrigerator and cut dough in half. Roll out each piece to fit a 9-inch pie pan. Line pan with dough and pleat edges. Poke holes in bottom and sides of crust.

Preheat oven to 350 degrees. In a large bowl, combine all filling ingredients together and whip until smooth. Pour into uncooked pie shells. Cover pie with foil to prevent burning of crust while pie is cooking. Bake for 20 to 30 minutes; remove foil once pie filling is solid, and bake until edges are brown. Cool and serve.

Chapter 8

PRIZEWINNERS

Wichita foodies love a little competition.

Some have won recipe contests sponsored by food companies or wineries, walking away with thousands of dollars in prize money. Others have become regulars on the chili and barbecue cookoff circuits, winning enough to qualify for events like the American Royal World Series of Barbecue in Kansas City. A few have made their way onto nationally televised cooking shows.

Here are recipes from some who have taken home prizes. After all, everyone loves a winner.

Jason Febres carves jambon at Taste and See, a restaurant he owned in Old Town. Febres was a three-peat winner of the Orpheum Theatre's Celebrity & Chef Cookoff before going on to compete in nationally televised food shows.

Mocha Rocky Road Oatmeal Cookies

Julie Veith won $10,000 from Quaker Oats for this recipe, named "Oatmeal Cookie of the Millennium." Yeah, they're that good.
Makes about 2 dozen cookies.
Source: Julie Veith

1 cup (2 sticks) butter, softened
½ cup firmly packed brown sugar
½ cup granulated sugar
2 eggs
1 ½ teaspoons vanilla
1 tablespoon instant coffee granules
1 tablespoon hot water
1 ¾ cups all-purpose flour (see notes)
1 teaspoon baking soda
½ teaspoon salt
2½ cups quick-cooking or old-fashioned oats, uncooked (see notes)
1 ½ cups semisweet chocolate chips
1 ½ cups coarsely chopped toasted walnuts
1 ½ cups miniature marshmallows

Heat oven to 350 degrees. Spray cookie sheets with cooking spray.

In a large bowl, beat butter and sugars with electric mixer until creamy. Add eggs and vanilla; beat well. Dissolve coffee granules in hot water. Add to butter mixture; mix well. Add combined flour, baking soda and salt; mix well. Stir in oats, chocolate chips and walnuts. To shape cookies, flatten 1 heaping tablespoon of dough in palm of hand. Arrange 4 marshmallows on top; wrap dough around marshmallows to completely cover. Repeat with remaining dough and marshmallows. Space cookies 2 inches apart on cookie sheets. Bake 10 to 12 minutes or until edges are golden brown. Do not overbake; centers of cookies should be soft.

Let stand 2 minutes on cookie sheets; remove to wire racks. Cool completely. Store tightly covered.

Notes: For old-fashioned oats, add 2 additional tablespoons flour. Instant coffee granules may be omitted.

Shrimp Bruschetta with Guacamole

Olga Esquivel-Holman was a finalist in several national recipe contests
and won $10,000 from *Southern Living* magazine for this one.
Source: Olga Esquivel-Holman

24 unpeeled, uncooked, fresh or frozen large shrimp
1 (16-ounce) French bread baguette
Nonstick cooking spray
2 large avocados
2 teaspoons fresh lime juice
½ teaspoon salt
¼ teaspoon ground cumin
1 garlic clove, finely chopped
1 tablespoon shallot, diced
¼ cup medium salsa
½ cup fresh cilantro, chopped
2 garlic cloves, finely chopped
¼ cup extra-virgin olive oil
¾ cup freshly grated Manchego cheese
Garnish: 12 fresh cilantro sprigs

If frozen, thaw shrimp according to package directions. Peel shrimp
and, if desired, devein. Set aside.

Cut bread diagonally into 12 (½-inch-thick) slices, discarding ends.
Coat both sides with cooking spray and place on a baking sheet. Bake
at 375 degrees for 5 to 6 minutes or until edges are crisp. Reserve
bread on pan.

Peel and coarsely chop avocados and place in a medium bowl. Add
lime juice and next 6 ingredients and gently combine, being careful to
retain small avocado chunks. (Do not mash.) Chill until ready to serve.

Sauté garlic in hot oil in a medium skillet over medium heat for 1
minute. Add shrimp, in batches, and cook 2 minutes on each side or
just until shrimp turn pink. (Shrimp should be slightly undercooked.)
Remove from pan and place 2 shrimp on top of each baguette slice on
baking sheet. Top each with 1 tablespoon Manchego cheese.

Broil 5 inches from heat 1 to 2 minutes or until cheese melts.
Remove from oven and top each with 1 to 2 tablespoons avocado
mixture. Garnish, if desired. Serve immediately.

Bittersweet Chocolate Cake Rounds

Rick Finney was the first male to win the Kansas State Fair's "King of the Kitchen Award," entering 129 different categories one year and winning two more blue ribbons than the nearest finisher. Here's a recipe he modeled on a dessert he enjoyed at a Boston-area restaurant. It's a little more complicated than some flourless cakes, but it's also the best I ever tasted.

Source: Rick Finney

Cake:

½ cup sugar, plus 2 tablespoons
⅓ cup water
3 ounces premium bittersweet chocolate, such as Scharffen Berger, roughly chopped
3½ ounces premium unsweetened chocolate, such as Scharffen Berger, roughly chopped
9 tablespoons unsalted butter, cubed
3 large eggs, at room temperature
Boiling water

Sauce:

3 ounces premium bittersweet chocolate
½ cup heavy cream
Cocoa powder for garnish

Preheat oven to 300 degrees. Generously butter 4 (8-ounce) or 6 (6-ounce) ramekins and set aside.

Place ½ cup sugar and water in a small saucepan and bring to a boil. Combine chocolate and butter in a medium bowl and pour boiling sugar solution over, stirring to melt chocolate and butter.

In a separate bowl, combine the eggs and remaining 2 tablespoons of sugar and whip with an electric mixer or by hand until foamy and soft peaks almost form. Gently fold egg mixture into chocolate one-third at a time and divide among ramekins. Place in a roasting pan to which you add boiling water to come three-fourths of the way to the top of the ramekins. (It is easier and safer to place the pan on the oven rack first and then add water.) Bake 30 to 40 minutes or until a toothpick comes out with just a few crumbs on it. Remove from water bath and cool on rack to room temperature.

Prepare sauce by combining the first two ingredients in a small pan over low heat until blended.

Gently remove cakes from ramekins by sliding a knife around outside edges and gently shaking upside down in your hand. These are very delicate cakes. Serve on small plates dusted with cocoa powder, topped with ice cream and drizzled with chocolate sauce.

Grilled Prosciutto-Wrapped Asparagus

College student Dan Myers won an all-expenses-paid trip to California, a spot on a Food Network show and a chance to meet boxer George Foreman with this recipe, prepared for a contest sponsored by the company that makes George Foreman grills.

Source: Dan Myers

Grilled Prosciutto-Wrapped Asparagus makes a great side or appetizer.

4 slices prosciutto
12 stalks asparagus, trimmed
Olive oil
Kosher salt, freshly ground black pepper and cayenne pepper to taste

Preheat George Foreman grill to 350 degrees (if temperature setting is available).

Roll prosciutto around groups of three asparagus stalks. Brush bundles with olive oil and season with salt, pepper and cayenne.

Grill bundles about 5 minutes or until asparagus is soft.

Peanut Butter Cookie Candy Bars
This recipe landed Amy Wood in the finals of the nationwide Betty Crocker "Bake Life Sweeter" contest. She donated $1,500 in box tops she won to an elementary school.
Source: Amy Wood

Cooking spray

Cookie Dough Crust:
1 pouch (1 pound, 1.5 ounces) Betty Crocker peanut butter cookie mix
1 tablespoon water
3 tablespoons vegetable oil
1 egg

Nougat Layer:
1 ½ tablespoons water
⅓ cup light corn syrup
3 tablespoons butter
1 ¼ teaspoons vanilla extract
3 tablespoons peanut butter
Dash salt
3 ½ cups powdered sugar

Caramel Layer:
1 bag (14 ounces) caramels, unwrapped
2 tablespoons water
1 ½ cups dry-roasted unsalted peanuts

Topping:
1 bag (11.5 ounces) milk chocolate chips

Heat oven to 350 degrees. Spray bottom of 13x9-inch pan with cooking spray. Make cookie dough as directed on pouch, adding water, vegetable oil and egg.

Press dough into pan. Bake 12 to 15 minutes or until edges are light golden brown. Cool to touch.

In a large bowl, beat 1 ½ tablespoons water, corn syrup, butter, vanilla, peanut butter and salt with electric mixer on medium speed until creamy. Slowly add powdered sugar. When nougat is the consistency of dough, press evenly over cookie crust. Set pan in refrigerator.

Melt caramels in a small saucepan with 2 tablespoons water over low heat. Once melted, stir in peanuts. Pour the mixture evenly over the nougat layer. Cool in the refrigerator, about 15 minutes.

When the caramel mixture is firm, melt milk chocolate chips in an uncovered, small microwavable bowl on medium-high (70 percent) for 1 minute. Stir. Microwave for 20 additional seconds as needed, then stir. Continue until melted and smooth. Once melted, pour evenly over caramel layer. Cool completely until chocolate is set (bars can be refrigerated to speed up the cooling process). Cut into bars. Store covered at room temperature.

*Baked Olives

These addictive nibbles helped Jane Hodge of Wichita win the five-ingredients-or-less recipe contest we held for the *Eagle*'s food section. They are easy to prep ahead of time and then pop into the oven just before guests arrive.

Source: Jane Hodge

Tube of crescent roll dough (8-roll size)
2-ounce jar small pimiento-stuffed green olives, drained and patted dry
Olive oil
Chopped rosemary
Freshly ground black pepper

Pinch or cut off dough and wrap around each olive. Seal well and place seam side down on baking sheet. Mist or brush with oil. Sprinkle with chopped rosemary and pepper. Bake at 400 degrees about 10 to 15 minutes or until golden.

Greek Pasta with Tomatoes and White Beans

This dish from Dedra Sinclair of Derby was another winner in the
Eagle's five-ingredients-or-less recipe contest. It boasts a lot of flavor
for very little work.
Makes 4 servings.
Source: Dedra Sinclair

2 cans (14.5 ounces each) diced tomatoes with basil, garlic and oregano
1 can (15.5 ounces) cannellini or other white beans, rinsed and drained
1 bag (10 ounces) fresh spinach, chopped
½ pound cooked penne pasta
½ cup finely crumbled feta cheese

Combine tomatoes and beans in a large nonstick skillet over medium-
high heat; bring to a boil. Reduce heat; simmer 10 minutes. Add spinach,
cooking 2 minutes or until it wilts, stirring occasionally. Divide pasta,
sauce and cheese among four plates.

Blue Ribbon Pie

Linda Pauls of Buhler won a blue ribbon at the Kansas State Fair with this
pie, which is unusual in that it includes two kinds of fruit.
Source: Linda Pauls

4 cups sliced fresh or frozen peaches
1½ cups sugar mixed with 2 dashes each of nutmeg and cinnamon
3 tablespoons cornstarch
2 (9-inch) refrigerated pie crusts
1 can (11 ounces) mandarin oranges (use about 12 slices)
2 teaspoons honey
1 tablespoon butter

Optional glaze:
1 egg and an equal amount of vegetable oil

Mix the peaches with sugar, nutmeg, cinnamon and cornstarch; set
aside. Thaw the crusts as directed on package. Line a 9-inch pie plate

with bottom crust, add the peaches, then top with the mandarin orange segments in a circle about 1 inch from the center. Drizzle with honey and dot with butter. Prepare the top crust by cutting slits or decorations and put over the filling, sealing the edges well. Put on the glaze if desired and sprinkle lightly with sugar. Bake in a preheated 450-degree oven for 10 minutes, then turn down heat to 350 degrees and continue baking for 30 minutes more or until golden brown. Tent with foil if browning too fast.

Pepper Mike's Chili

Haysville construction worker Mike Simpson grew as many as eighty varieties of chiles while competing in chili and barbecue cookoffs. If you don't love heat as much as Pepper Mike, reduce the amount of chiles called for in the recipe.
Source: Mike Simpson

½ medium white onion
½ medium red onion
½ red bell pepper
2 jalapeño peppers, seeds removed
2 hot Portugal peppers, seeds removed
1 stalk celery (optional)
1 pound ground beef
1 pound ground pork
About 7 tablespoons chili seasoning (see recipe below)
1 pound sausage
2 cups canned crushed tomatoes
1 ½ cups spicy tomato juice
⅔ cup tomato juice
½ cup beef broth
1 can (16 ounces) dark red kidney beans
1 can (16 ounces) light red kidney beans
1 can (16 ounces) black beans
2 habaneros (optional)

Chop the onions, peppers and celery, keeping them separate. In a skillet, brown the ground beef with the onions (and celery, if used), drain and put into a large pot. Brown pork with 1 tablespoon chili seasoning. Add the sausage to the pot and brown; add crushed tomato, bell pepper, tomato juices, beef broth, jalapeño and Portugal peppers and 4 to 6 tablespoons chili seasoning. While this is heating, drain 3 cans of beans. Add beans to the chili just after it starts to simmer. While bringing the temperature back up, stir the chili carefully so as not to break down the beans. After about 20 minutes, taste and add chopped habanero to taste. Add more beef broth or tomato juice if mixture is too thick.

To make the chili seasoning, combine: 1½ teaspoons ground black pepper, 1½ teaspoons seasoned salt, 3 tablespoons paprika, 5 tablespoons chili powder, 1½ teaspoons cayenne pepper, 1½ tablespoons cumin, 1½ teaspoons crushed red pepper and 1½ teaspoons garlic powder. Store any leftover mixture in an airtight container.

Note: Mike Simpson prefers to use coarsely ground beef and pork in this chili. Ask your butcher if they're available. If you don't add beans to the chili, leave out 1½ tablespoons chili seasoning.

Mindy's Bierock Casserole
Mindy Wooten of Halstead won the Active Age's first holiday recipe contest with this take on that old-time Kansas favorite, the bierock. Her recipe delivers the flavor of the original with much less work.
Source: Mindy Wooten

1 pound ground beef
2 teaspoons garlic, minced
½ large onion, chopped
½ head cabbage, finely chopped
2 tablespoons soy sauce
1 package Lipton onion soup mix
2 cups water (add more if necessary)
2 cups instant rice
Salt and pepper, to taste
1½ cups grated cheddar cheese
1 package crescent rolls

Brown ground beef with garlic and onion; drain liquid.

Add cabbage, soy sauce, onion soup mix and water, simmering until cabbage is cooked. Add instant rice, cover and let sit until liquid is absorbed by rice (you may need to add water). Season with salt and pepper as needed.

Pour into 9x13 pan and top with cheddar cheese.

Roll out crescent rolls in one big sheet to top the pan. Roll between two sheets of wax paper that have been sprayed with cooking spray. Peel off top sheet of wax paper, then place dough facedown on top of casserole and peel off bottom sheet.

Bake at 375 degrees until crust is very brown, about 20 to 25 minutes. Let sit about 5 minutes, then cut into squares and serve.

Mediterranean Quesadillas

Eagle reader Teresa Williams's fusion of Mediterranean and Mexican cuisine won first place in the newspaper's 2007 holiday cookbook contest. The cookbook was a tradition for half a century. Thousands of entries were submitted in the early years; evaluating and testing recipes became the food editor's full-time job for part of the year. Later, reader participation tapered off, but the cookbook remained a popular feature.
Source: Teresa Williams

Butter, enough to spread thinly on tortillas
8 10-inch flour tortillas
2 packages (8 ounces each) Mediterranean-style Kraft Natural Crumbles
½ cup kalamata olives, pitted and chopped
1 pound frozen spinach, thawed, rinsed and dried in kitchen towel
1 medium red onion, sliced thinly

Cucumber Sauce:
1 cup sour cream
1 medium cucumber, peeled and chopped
1–2 tablespoons fresh lemon juice

For quesadillas, place 10-inch sauté pan over medium heat. Butter one tortilla and place, buttered side down, in pan. Spread about ½ cup of cheese on tortilla, followed by ¼ of the olives, ¼ of the spinach and

¼ of the onion. Top with ½ cup more cheese and another buttered tortilla.

Cook on medium 3 to 4 minutes or until golden brown before flipping. Flip and cook until golden brown on both sides. Repeat with remaining tortillas and ingredients. Allow quesadilla to cool before cutting. Cut into 8 pie shapes with pizza cutter.

For sauce, combine all ingredients in a bowl. Serve with quesadillas.

Chicken with Bow Tie Pasta

When Stouffer's held a nationwide contest to find a new frozen food entry, Marie Elliott's recipe made it to the final ten out of three thousand submitted. She gave all credit to her mom, Kay Martin, who'd brought over the dish soon after Elliott gave birth to twin daughters.

Source: Marie Elliott

Marinade:

¼ cup olive oil
2 tablespoons lemon juice
4 cloves garlic, minced
1 tablespoon Worcestershire sauce
1 teaspoon dried thyme
1 teaspoon dried basil
¼ teaspoon oregano
1 teaspoon salt
Dash freshly ground pepper
1 pound chicken breast, cut into 1-inch pieces

10–12 ounces pasta
1 pound bacon

Sauce:

⅔ cup sherry
1½ cups half-and-half
⅔ cup grated Parmesan cheese
Freshly ground pepper, to taste

¾ cup green onions, sliced, including tops

Three to twenty-four hours before cooking, mix all marinade ingredients together in order given. Pour over chicken pieces. Put all in a sealed container in the refrigerator.

Prepare pasta according to package directions.

While pasta is cooking, fry and crumble bacon. Coat 12-inch skillet with nonstick spray. Heat to high. Pour chicken and marinade into skillet. Cook thoroughly, stirring occasionally.

For sauce, heat sherry to boiling in a small saucepan. Boil until alcohol has cooked out, about 2 minutes. Remove from heat. Add half-and-half and cheese. Stir to mix thoroughly. Cook over medium heat until warm and cheese is melted, about 5 minutes. Add pepper to taste.

To serve, assemble on a large dish in this order: pasta, chicken, sauce, bacon and green onion.

Paella

Chef Jason Febres appeared on nationally televised shows such as *Guy's Grocery Games* and *Cutthroat Kitchen* while owning Taste and See restaurant. He later started Rent the Chef, cooking for private events and parties. I love his paella, which he keeps juicy by adding a little broth to it just before serving.

Makes 4 servings.

Source: Jason Febres

2 tablespoons butter
2 tablespoons olive oil
¼ onion, julienned
¼ red bell pepper, diced
2 garlic cloves, minced
Pinch saffron
½ cup dry white wine
8 cups warm chicken broth, plus 1–2 cups more for use at end
Salt, to taste
4 cups white rice
2 smoked andouille sausages (about 8 ounces), sliced
8 jumbo shrimp, peeled
8 mussels

Seafood,
Chicken
and Sausage
Paella.

1 cooked chicken breast, meat pulled (can use rotisserie chicken)
2 cups broccoli florets
¼ cup peas
2 tablespoons chopped cilantro, plus 4 springs for garnish
1 lime, cut into 4 wedges

In a large pan with lid or Dutch oven, heat butter and olive oil over medium-high heat. Sauté onion and pepper until onion is slightly browned. Add garlic and saffron and cook 20 seconds. Deglaze immediately with wine. Add 8 cups of stock, a pinch of salt and rice. Bring to a boil. Add sausage, shrimp, mussels, chicken, broccoli and peas. Reduce heat to medium and cover.

Cook until liquid is evaporated and rice is done.

Add stock until rice is juicy but not soupy. Add cilantro and season to taste with salt.

To serve, scoop rice onto plates or into bowls, arrange proteins and vegetables on top, then garnish with lime wedges and cilantro sprigs. For heat, sprinkle with red pepper flakes.

Turtle Espresso Martini

This recipe from Caffé Moderne in Old Town Square won a cocktail
contest in Kansas City.
Source: Caffé Moderne

Caramel sauce
½ cup finely crushed pecans (you probably won't need all of them)
1 shot espresso or strong coffee, room temperature
1 ½ shots chocolate-flavored vodka
½ shot creme de cocoa
½ shot Baileys caramel-flavored Irish creme
1 scoop chocolate gelato
¼ cup ice cubes
Chocolate syrup

Rim a martini glass with caramel sauce by spreading caramel sauce on
a plate and inverting the glass onto the plate. Place the crushed pecans
on a plate and invert the caramel-rimmed glasses onto the plate until
the nuts stick to the glass.

In a blender, combine the espresso, chocolate-flavored vodka, creme
de cocoa, Baileys, gelato and ice cubes. Blend until smooth.

Pour mixture into prepared martini glass. Squirt chocolate sauce
and a little more caramel sauce onto surface of the martini, sprinkle
with more crushed pecans and serve.

Chapter 9

RIP

For almost two decades, Tanya Tandoc was Wichita's best-known restaurant owner. That's true even when she wasn't in the restaurant business. During the eight-year period between the first and second incarnations of Tanya's Soup Kitchen, it seemed that all anyone wanted to know was: When will she open another restaurant?

When I met Tanya, her restaurant was located just out the back door from the *Wichita Eagle*, in the former Union Station baggage building. Two things impressed me: the volume of tattoos she sported (not quite as common then as now) and the amount of heavy cream she put in many of her soups.

"Cream is love," she purred, punctuating the remark with a giggle. She was always very quotable.

At the time, Tanya wasn't interested in having anything written about her. It wasn't that she shunned the spotlight; she'd already received plenty of love from local journalists. Instead, she insisted I meet her neighbor Norma Sowell, who grew herbs for the Soup Kitchen in her backyard near Douglas and Hillside. As we toured her backyard garden, I asked Tanya something along the lines of, "Why go to all the trouble and expense of growing fresh herbs when the bottled kind work just fine?" I can't remember her reply, but I'm sure it was amusing and unprintable.

Tanya exerted a huge influence on the city's food community, and not just in the educating of one newbie food editor. She held cooking classes. She worked as a consultant for Cargill and restaurants. Many Wichitans cook from the sets of recipe cards she sold each Christmas.

Tanya Tandoc, seen here sampling a shrimp boil at her restaurant, rarely had anything uninteresting to say about food. *Courtesy of Tanya's Soup Kitchen.*

Tanya often served as a judge at cookoffs. She had an uncanny ability to taste a dish, decipher just what ingredients were in it and then describe it in the most appealing terms possible. On public radio station KMUW, she reviewed local restaurants, sending them waves of new customers. She seemed incapable of saying anything boring about food.

She wasn't all warm and fuzzy. She told me once that her restaurant staff had to "drink the Kool-Aid" in order to work for her. She cussed Cox Communications for evicting her from her first location and said city officials were no help. Her closest friends were other strong, independent female business owners in the hospitality industry.

Our paths often crossed, usually at events involving music or food. She was definitely in charge when we teamed up for a celebrity-chef cookoff benefiting the Orpheum Theatre. Despite producing lovely rosemary/goat cheese/strawberry crepes, we did not win.

One night, we hosted Tanya and her husband at the time, musician Wayne Gottstine, for dinner. Afterward, I realized with horror that we had served them soup and bread pudding, the two things for which Tanya was most celebrated. But she said that people in her business were happy just to be invited to anybody's home for dinner.

Food was far from Tanya's only interest. When her first restaurant closed in 2004, she earned a fine arts degree at Wichita State University. She played the cello and became a sort of pied piperess of belly dance in the city, teaching at a studio and staging "flash dances" around town. She loved animals and was known to deliver soup to sick friends.

She reopened the Soup Kitchen on East Douglas in 2012. Three years later, she was murdered by an acquaintance she had let live in her basement. But she won't be forgotten by anyone who crossed her passionate, irreverent, infectious path.

NEIGHBORLY TYPE

Chuck Giles, who built Neighbors Bar & Restaurant into a thriving west-side eatery, was kind of the anti-Tanya. In fact, he didn't like her. Or rather, he disliked the way local media fawned over her, seemingly keeping her on speed dial for whenever a quote was needed about food or the restaurant business. That was Chuck's curmudgeonly side, which he never tried to hide. The truth is, both were full of strong opinions and capable of expressing them in colorful ways.

Chuck had been in the food business since his high school days working for a Sonic Drive-In in Atchison. He moved to Wichita to manage a Denny's. He took a job at Chi-Chi's, then ran the Wichita location of Stroud's, where he learned to make its famous pan-fried chicken. Eventually, Chuck's version surpassed the original (in my opinion), and I was a happy man indeed when he shared his chicken-frying technique with me. "It ain't brain surgery," he said.

In 2002, Chuck and an investor, Red, bought the former KC's restaurant in the Twin Lakes shopping center and renamed it Neighbors. Red helped Chuck with the business side of things, and Chuck looked after Red until his death. Neighbors quickly became known for its pan-fried chicken, chicken-fried steak, cheeseburgers, steaks and huge breakfasts. Chuck's strategy was to serve big portions of tasty food at a very reasonable price, so it's not surprising that it became the kind of place people ate at over and over. It was, they said, like eating at home. Except with better food.

Chuck Giles's last stop of the night often was the supermarket as he picked up supplies for the next day's business at Neighbors. *Photo by Carrie Rengers.*

Chuck put in ridiculously long hours at Neighbors. Usually, he'd be there before sunup to start breakfast, work through the lunch hour, go home for a nap and then return for the dinner rush.

At Neighbors, every piece of fried chicken was hand-breaded before being lowered into a cast-iron skillet full of hot grease. Chuck could keep five or six skillets full of chicken frying at the same time he oversaw a grill full of steaks and burgers while simultaneously complaining about the Kansas City Royals' pitching staff or some boneheaded move a local politician had made.

Chuck was just as old school when it came to the business side of things. He kept most of it in his head and carried around too much money, as if his pocket was a cash register. He could be a tough boss. But he also hired cooks out of work-release and other people who needed work and helped them get back on their feet, making them loans and advances on their pay when they needed money for rent or a car.

Despite his bouts of irascibility, Chuck actually loved taking off his apron and getting to know customers. He was intensely interested in current events and seemed to know something about just about everything that was going on in Wichita, both from paying attention to news reports and from his big network of customers who'd become friends.

At times, Chuck talked about taking Neighbors in a more upscale direction. That never happened, probably to the relief of customers. Both his daughter, Ashley, and longtime companion, Connie, were key parts of the operation.

In 2015, Chuck moved Neighbors around the corner to its current location on West 21st Street. It became even more popular, with lines out the door. Chuck was a lot better at taking care of customers than taking care of himself. Not long after moving his restaurant, he collapsed in a diabetic coma and nearly died. It took him a long time to recover. But eventually he was back to working fifteen- and sixteen-hour days.

Chuck's habit of carrying around large amounts of cash—he was fond of the Kansas Star Casino—probably got him killed. He left work on the night of July 19, 2019, stopped at a nearby Dillons supermarket and then continued on to his home a short distance away in Benjamin Hills. After pulling into his driveway, Chuck was shot and robbed by one or more people in what police called a "targeted event." No arrest had been made as of this writing.

I was honored to speak at his funeral. I brought along a cast-iron skillet. I think Chuck would have appreciated the attempt at levity. But truthfully, I did it because Chuck used ones like it to create a place where people actually did feel like they were visiting a neighbor, which is not a bad legacy.

Tanya's Tomato Bisque
Source: Tanya Tandoc

1 can (28 ounces) crushed tomatoes, with juices
1 small can (6 ounces) tomato paste
1 cup water

2 cups heavy cream
2 teaspoons dried dill
1 teaspoon garlic powder
Salt and pepper, to taste
2 tablespoons sugar, or to taste

Put all ingredients in a pot and whisk together. Bring to a boil, reduce heat and simmer 10 minutes.

Sesame-Seared Scallops on Tomato Curry Cream
Tanya Tandoc prepared this dish for a California winemakers' dinner at her restaurant. It was paired with a Riesling.
Makes 3–4 servings.
Source: Tanya Tandoc

1 pound large scallops
6 tablespoons sesame seeds, toasted
2 teaspoons cumin seeds, toasted
½ cup flour
½ teaspoon salt
¼ teaspoon black pepper
½ cup milk
Vegetable oil for frying

Tomato Curry:
2 tablespoons butter
½ medium onion, minced
4 cloves garlic, minced
1 tablespoon ginger, minced
3 Roma tomatoes, seeded and diced
1 teaspoon curry powder
1 cup heavy cream
1–2 teaspoons sugar
1 teaspoon lemon juice
Salt and pepper, to taste
Chopped scallions or green onions, for garnish

Wash scallops and pat dry.

To toast sesame and cumin seeds, place in a heavy-bottom skillet over medium heat and cook, stirring frequently, about 5 minutes. Do not burn.

In a bowl, mix toasted sesame and cumin seeds, flour, salt and pepper. Dip scallops in milk, then roll in flour mixture until coated with flour and seeds.

Heat oil over medium-high heat and fry scallops in several batches, turning once, about 3 minutes on each side or until done. Remove from heat, cover and keep warm.

To make tomato curry cream, melt butter over medium heat. Add onion and sauté about 5 minutes or until soft, adding garlic and ginger during last minute of cooking. Add tomatoes and cook several minutes, then add curry powder, cream, sugar and lemon juice, simmering until sauce thickens. Season with salt and pepper. Place sauce on plate, top with scallops and garnish with chopped scallions.

*Neighbors Pan-Fried Chicken
Source: Chuck Giles

Vegetable oil, for frying
1 whole chicken, the smaller the better, cut into 8 pieces
1 cup flour
1 teaspoon salt
½ teaspoon black pepper
¼ teaspoon cayenne pepper

In a large heavy-bottom skillet, heat vegetable oil over medium heat until it reaches 350 degrees.

Meanwhile, rinse chicken pieces and pat dry.

Combine flour, salt, black pepper and cayenne pepper in a bowl.

Dredge chicken pieces in flour mixture and place in hot oil. Allow enough room so that pieces don't touch. The oil should come halfway up the sides of the chicken. If it's too high, carefully spoon out a little.

Cook for 10 minutes, then turn pieces and cook for 10 more minutes. Remove cooked chicken to paper towel–lined plate, cover to keep warm and repeat with any remaining chicken.

Chapter 10

TO YOUR HEALTH

A good martini is like a sharp blow to the back of the neck.
—Hunter S. Thompson

We've covered a lot of Wichita's culinary ground and aren't quite done yet. So how about pausing for a refreshing adult beverage?

I was a beer-and-shot man when I arrived in Wichita. Then one evening while sitting in a bar, I heard another customer order a martini. I decided to give it a try.

Shake, shake, shake that martini!

Unlike the quote above, from one of my favorite writers, I found a martini to be more like a gentle massage of my nervous system. The first sip was crisp, cool and nearly odorless, as if it wanted to leave no trace. Subsequent sips did nothing to decrease my appreciation. I was determined to get to the bottom of martinis, in every sense of the word. And with practice and advice from a lot of Wichita bartenders (you know who you are), I concocted the:

*Perfect Dry Martini

Ice
Water
Gin (vodka is acceptable, but gin is better)
Extra-dry vermouth
Olive

Equipment:
Martini glass
Cocktail shaker

Fill martini glass with ice, then fill in the gaps with water. At this point, you are chilling the glass and in no particular hurry. If you are playing bartender at home, take somebody else's order.

When the glass is chilled, fill the cocktail shaker with ice, then pour the amount of gin you'll need to fill the martini glass into the cocktail shaker. Use a spare martini glass to gauge the right amount.

Close the cocktail shaker and shake it hard, up and down, for 10 seconds. This is longer than you imagine, and if your cocktail shaker is made of metal, the outside will be covered with a lovely winter morning–like frost by the time you're done. Unless you enjoy metal sticking to your skin, you may want to grip it with a towel.

Set the cocktail shaker down, pick up the martini glass by the stem and pour out the ice and water. Working quickly, tip a teaspoon or so of vermouth into the glass, swirl it around and then pour it back out, leaving only a film behind. Set down the martini glass, pick up the cocktail shaker and give it exactly five more shakes.

Uncover the cocktail shaker and strain its contents into the glass. If you've done it correctly, there should be tiny shards of ice floating on the surface, as in some pristine arctic sea (if not, shake a little longer next time). Plop in an olive and present it to your grateful self or guest.

But perhaps your tastes run in a different direction. You're in luck. Wichita is full of great watering holes. Here are recipes from a few.

Mort's: Cucumber Bloody Mary
Mort's is famous for its live music, year-round patio
and cocktails such as this one.

1 ¼ ounces cucumber-infused vodka (homemade or a brand such as Effen)
2 tablespoons olive juice
1 tablespoon Worcestershire sauce

2 teaspoons vinegar-based hot sauce (such as Frank's)
¼ teaspoon pepper blend (look for one containing garlic)
About 3 ounces V8 juice

Place ice, vodka and seasonings in a 12- to 16-ounce glass with ice; add V8, about 3 ounces, until filled. Mix well by tumbling into another glass (or using a cocktail shaker). Garnish with fresh cucumber, pickles or your favorite pickled vegetables.

Brickyard: Creamsicle
An open-air bar with attached restaurant, the Brickyard offers hours of dining, drinking and dancing possibilities.

1 ounce Stolichnaya orange-flavored vodka
1 ounce Licor 43
Splash half-and-half
½ cup ice
1 scoop orange sherbet or other ice cream

Combine ingredients in blender until slushy.

YaYa's: Sweetheart Champagne Cocktail
Veteran mixologist Paula Topping came up with this cocktail for those hot summer nights on the patio.
Source: YaYa's

4 fresh basil leaves, cut into thin strips
5 fresh strawberries
½ ounce simple syrup (see note)
1 ounce Grand Marnier or other orange-flavored liqueur
Favorite champagne or sparkling wine

In a cocktail shaker, muddle together basil leaves, 4 strawberries and simple syrup. Add Grand Marnier, then pour mixture over ice in a tall wine glass. Top with champagne, garnish with remaining strawberry and serve.

Note: to make simple syrup, heat equal parts sugar and water in a saucepan until sugar is dissolved. Leftover syrup can be refrigerated for up to a month.

Vorshay Nights

Craft cocktails and live entertainment are the draws at Vorshay's, housed in a historic former downtown movie theater.
Source: Vorshay's

1 ounce simple syrup
1 ounce lemon juice
1 ounce mango aloe water
3 ounces Redrum (a brand of infused rum)

Combine ingredients in a cocktail. Serve over ice, garnished with a lemon twist.

Chapter 11

NEXT COURSE

I'm writing this during the coronavirus pandemic that's disrupted Wichita's food scene and just about everything else. Accordingly, this chapter, on what might lie ahead for that scene, is even more speculative than it might have been. Some restaurants have closed because of the crisis. Others have opened. Home cooking enjoyed a renaissance, judging from social media, where users' discovery of their ovens was regularly celebrated.

I proceed from two assumptions:

1.) People must eat.

2.) Some people will continue to enjoy cooking and serving great food.

Prior to the pandemic, Wichita's dining landscape seemed to be in a good place, with even better times ahead. All those things I mentioned in the introduction—the Eat Local movement, creative chefs, food trucks, top-notch beer and coffee—were happening here. There was a sense of collaboration, as seen in events like the food truck rallies at WaterWalk organized by Flying Stove owners Jeff and Rob Schauf. "We wanted to be like a community," Jeff told me.

Central Standard Brewing, Nortons, Hopping Gnome and other brewpubs conducted themselves more as allies battling Budweiser and Coors than competitors vying against one another; they'd lend each other a bag of barley or hops in a pinch. Restaurants such as the Anchor and Public at the Brickyard put the beer of local brewpubs on their taps even though those brewpubs compete for some of the same drinking dollars.

Jeff and Rob Schauf returned to Wichita to get the food truck scene rolling with the Flying Stove. Today, the city is home to dozens of four-wheeled kitchens.

Schane Gross, who owns the Anchor and its meat market next door, enjoys collaborating with colleagues in the industry, saying she'd get bored otherwise.

Left: Cooking classes such as this one at Mark Arts are a popular way for home cooks to expand their culinary skills.

Right: Megan Greenway and Wes Johnson (not shown) of Orie's Farm Fresh grow a variety of vegetables in northwest Wichita. They're best known for their prodigious garlic crop. Typically, they raise about thirty varieties, totaling nearly twenty thousand bulbs annually.

There also seemed to be a growing appreciation for what Wichita has to offer. Sometimes it stemmed from outsiders—say, Alton Brown of Food Network fame or your college buddies in town for a wedding—raving about something they've eaten or drunk here. It's registered with many residents that Wichita offers a laidback, affordable lifestyle that visitors envy.

Hopefully that's all restarted by the time you read this.

Where else is the city headed in terms of food?

The Eat Local movement will doubtless continue to expand as purveyors and their customers multiply. Firefly Farm, near Andover, started supplying organically grown heirloom tomatoes and a few other summer crops to three restaurants in 2015. By 2020, it was raising and selling food year-round and had added nearly twenty restaurants as clients. Firefly stages its own autumnal farm-to-fork dinners with guest chefs.

In Kechi, Elderslie Farm makes several varieties of cheese from its own goats, selling it at farmers' markets and in specialty stores from here to Denver. At the farm, a small outdoor café serves breakfast and lunch

Left: Leon Eames adds roux to a vat of étouffée for the Cajun Food Fest held during Riverfest. Wichita chefs and restaurants donate their time and food to numerous charitable events.

Right: Volunteers ready pork stew at the Lord's Diner, which serves free dinners every day of the year. Started in 2002 by the Catholic Diocese of Wichita, the operation has grown to two dining locations and three food trucks, with more than 5.5 million meals served. Hunger, food insecurity and food deserts in which people lack access to healthy food remain problems in Wichita.

throughout the summer, and upscale farm-to-table dinners are staged several nights a week.

Fidelity Bank is turning the roof of its new five-story parking garage into a five-thousand-square-foot urban farm touted as the largest of its kind in the Midwest. The city has mulled a Food System Master Plan designed to get more people growing and selling food.

To get around south central Kansas's limited growing season, more producers are turning to greenhouses and hydroponics. In south Wichita, Jimmy Vo's Kan-Gro Hydro Farm cranks out organic bean sprouts, microgreens and more for numerous restaurants; Vo is a cook in his own right, known for his restaurant pop-ups at Central Standard and elsewhere.

Marty Johnson of Johnson's Garden Centers has turned Hatch chiles into a local favorite by trucking them in from New Mexico and roasting them in his parking lot. Johnson's Iron ChiliHead Festival, an opportunity for local food trucks and brewers to incorporate Hatch chiles into their offerings, is one of the summer's most-anticipated parties.

By the time you read this, WSU Tech should be training chefs in a new culinary and hospitality program. Plans call for the school to locate in the old Henry's department store building downtown. John and Lexi Michael, who met at the Culinary Institute of America in Hyde Park, New York, and ran Butler Community College's culinary program for several years, will lead WSU Tech's new program.

Wichita continues to attract new culinary talent, drawn by opportunity and the city's aptitude for a good time. Veteran chefs and restaurateurs continue to try new things as well. Jeremy Wade, who ran kitchens at Uptown Bistro, YaYa's, the Candle Club and elsewhere, opened his own place, the Italian restaurant Napoli, in late 2020. I mentioned George Youssef's move into Georges Bistro and Chester's Chophouse earlier. John Arnold, who started as Redrock Canyon Grill's managing partner, continues to expand and tinker with a restaurant roster that includes Deano's Grill & Tapworks, Oak & Pie, Stearman Field & Bar and Jax.

And it should be a source of pride that Scott Redler, who had some success with Timberline Steakhouses back in the 2000s, joined with the Simon brothers to build Freddy's Frozen Custard & Steakburgers into one of the fastest-growing chains in the country with nearly four hundred locations before selling majority interest in it to a private equity firm in 2021. Not long after, Redler and his wife, Betsy, donated the money to build a new home for Butler Community College's culinary and hospitality program.

It's a lot of information to swallow. And yet somehow, I've worked up another appetite.

The Flying Stove: Chicken Doobie
Source: Rob Schauf, the Flying Stove

3 tablespoons vegetable oil
½ yellow onion, julienned
½ poblano, julienned
½ red bell pepper, julienned
6 boneless, skinless chicken thighs
2 tablespoons sambal (see note)
½ tablespoon fresh rosemary, minced

Chicken Doobie. *Courtesy of the Flying Stove.*

½ tablespoon fresh thyme, minced
Salt and pepper, to taste
3 cloves garlic, minced
1 lemon
1 cup Monterey Jack cheese
8 flour tortillas
Sriracha, to taste
Arugula

Heat 1 tablespoon oil in a large nonstick skillet over medium-high heat. Add onion, poblano and red bell pepper and cook, stirring occasionally, about 8 to 10 minutes or until onion starts to caramelize. Put in a bowl and set aside.

Put the boneless, skinless chicken thighs through a grinder. Add sambal to chicken and marinate in refrigerator at least 20 minutes.

When ready to cook, heat 2 tablespoons oil in the skillet over medium-high heat. Spread chicken evenly in skillet. Season with rosemary, thyme, salt and pepper. When chicken is brown on one side, use spatula to break up chicken, cooking for another 2 minutes. Move chicken to side of pan and add garlic to pan. Cook garlic about 30 seconds (add oil if necessary), then combine chicken and garlic in pan. Squeeze lemon over mixture. Put mixture in bowl, add Monterey Jack cheese and mix until creamy. Cover to keep warm.

Warm flour tortillas. Divide chicken mixture between tortillas, top with sriracha and arugula and serve.

Note: Sambal is an Indonesian chile paste sold in Asian markets and the Asian aisle of some supermarkets.

Roasted Garlic Honey Mustard

Use this sauce as a salad dressing, a dip for vegetables or bread and as a
base for tuna salad and other recipes calling for mayonnaise.

Source: Orie's Farm Fresh

1 cup neutral oil such as canola or grapeseed
Pinch of sea salt and ½ teaspoon, divided use
1 tablespoon white balsamic vinegar
1 egg, at room temperature (see note)
Freshly ground black pepper, to taste
2 tablespoons Dijon mustard
2–3 tablespoons honey
1 bulb roasted garlic (directions below)

Pour oil, pinch of sea salt and vinegar into a quart wide-mouth mason
jar. Crack in the egg.

Use a blender or whisk to thoroughly emulsify the oil and egg. The
mixture should be thick and creamy.

Add remaining sea salt, black pepper, Dijon mustard, honey and
roasted garlic to jar and blend again until thoroughly combined.
Refrigerate until ready to use.

How to roast garlic: Roasting garlic mellows its flavor and makes the
cloves soft enough to spread on bread. To roast garlic, preheat oven
to 375 degrees. Remove the outer papery bulb wrapper with your
fingers, then cut off about ¼ inch of the top of the bulb, revealing
the cloves. Cut a square of unbleached parchment and place garlic in
center. Drizzle a teaspoon of avocado or olive oil over the top of the
bulb, then wrap the parchment around the garlic and twist to seal shut
(placing the drizzled bulb in a ramekin covered by aluminum foil also
works). Place wrapped garlic bulb on a baking sheet and roast in the
oven for 30 to 45 minutes. Check for doneness after 30 minutes but
continue to roast until the cloves are golden and soft. The time will
vary depending on what variety of garlic you are using and how big the
cloves are.

Green Chile Burger

This burger is one of Marty Johnson's favorite summer grilling recipes. It can be made year-round as long as you've got chiles in the freezer.
Source: Marty Johnson

I pound 85/15 ground beef
½ cup onion, finely chopped
I egg, lightly beaten
I tablespoon grated Parmesan cheese
½ teaspoon salt
¼ teaspoon pepper
Mayonnaise
3 brioche hamburger buns
2 Hatch chiles, roasted, skinned, seeded and chopped
3 slices American cheese

Hatch chiles, trucked in from New Mexico and roasted, are a hot commodity in Wichita.

Combine first 6 ingredients; form into ⅓-pound patties and let set in refrigerator a couple of hours.

When ready to cook, heat grill to medium-high. Grill burgers about 6 minutes per side for medium-well (center should be about 160 degrees). Meanwhile, spread mayonnaise on inside surfaces of bun and grill until lightly toasted.

During last minute of cooking, top burgers with chopped chiles and cheese. Place burgers on buns and serve.

Spring Pea Hummus

Roger Cox is a well-traveled chef who moved to Wichita, left and returned. He created this dish as a seasonal appetizer while working as executive chef at Vora.
Source: Roger Cox

½ cup almonds, lightly toasted
2 tablespoons lemon juice, fresh squeezed
⅓ cup extra-virgin olive oil
¼ cup loosely packed mint leaves
⅓ cup water

1 teaspoon sea salt
4 cups fresh English peas, blanched for 1 minute in lightly salted boiling water (can
substitute frozen peas thawed but uncooked)
Dash or two of Tabasco

In blender, add almonds, lemon, olive oil, mint, water and salt. Puree until smooth. Add cooked peas and puree until smooth. If blender stalls, add small amounts of water a few teaspoons at a time until mixture starts moving again. Taste and add a few dashes of Tabasco and more salt if desired.

Serve garnished with chopped mint, a squeeze of lemon and a drizzle of extra-virgin olive oil with toast, crackers or vegetable crudité on the side.

Walnut River Barbecue Sauce

This barbecue sauce was created by Butler Community College culinary students for a farm-to-table dinner. It includes Warbeard Irish Red, brewed by the El Dorado–based Walnut River Brewing Co. It and the beer go great with pulled pork and other meat.
Source: John Michael

2 cups ketchup
3 tablespoons chile powder
12 ounces Warbeard Irish Red beer
1 teaspoon paprika
1 tablespoon garlic power
2 tablespoons yellow mustard
½ teaspoon cayenne
2 tablespoons brown sugar
2 tablespoons molasses
2 tablespoons apple cider vinegar

Combine all ingredients in a saucepan. Bring to a boil, then reduce heat and simmer about 10 minutes.

Sweet-spicy variation: substitute Teter Rock, a Kolsch-style beer made by Walnut River Brewing Co., for the Irish Red beer. Add 4 peaches, peeled and sliced, along with 2 jalapeños, seeded and minced, to the mixture before cooking.

Pesto Pasta Salad

Graduate student Lauren Overholt grew and prepared the ingredients in this dish as part of City Roots, one of the first concerted efforts to plant inner-city gardens in Wichita. Serve hot, cold or at room temperature.

Source: Lauren Overholt

Pesto:

4 cups gently packed basil
½ cup freshly grated Parmesan or Romano cheese
¾–1 cup olive oil
3 tablespoons pine nuts or walnuts
3 large cloves garlic, peeled and chopped
Salt and pepper, to taste

1 pound curly or bow-tie pasta, cooked according to package directions and drained
2 tomatoes, seeded and chopped
1 bell pepper, chopped

To make pesto, combine basil, Parmesan, olive oil, nuts and garlic in blender or food processor and blend until smooth. Season to taste with salt and pepper.

Toss cooked pasta with pesto, tomatoes and bell pepper. Garnish with ribbons of basil if desired.

Appendix A

RESOURCES

Most of the recipes in this book can be made with ingredients found in the supermarket. For other items, here are some ethnic markets and specialty stores you may find helpful.

ASIAN MARKETS

Grace Market, 1030 South Oliver
Kim Son, 960 East Pawnee
Lucky Market, 7100 East Harry
Thai Anh, 2425 South Hillside
Thai Binh, 1530 West 21st

Left: Kim Son, an Asian market on Pawnee, is known for its large tanks of live lobster and crab.

Right: An array of sauces and pastes comes in handy for Asian cooking.

Visit one of Wichita's tortillerias to find freshly made flour and corn tortillas still warm to the touch.

HISPANIC MARKETS

Carnaceria Ana, 2600 North Arkansas
El Rio Bravo Supermarket, 2501 South Seneca and 1989 West 21st
Juarez Bakery, 1068 North Waco
La Tienda Del Ahorro, 1770 North Broadway
La Tradicion Tortilleria, 1701 North Broadway
Super Del Centro, 2425 South Pawnee
Tortilla Rodriguez, 1859 North Waco

MIDDLE EASTERN MARKETS

Asia Bazaar, 6100 East 21st
Asian Groceries, 6249 East 21st
N&J Global Market, 5600 East Lincoln

SPECIALTY STORES

Nifty Nut House, 527 South St. Francis
The Spice Merchant, 1300 East Douglas

Appendix B

FAST-FOOD CAPITAL
OF THE UNIVERSE?

Air Capital of the World" has served Wichita well as a slogan. But I think it's time we lay claim to another part of our heritage: Fast-Food Capital of the Universe.

Why Wichita? Because the city has as good a claim as any to be the home of fast food. The two biggest sellers in the history of fast food—hamburgers and pizza—got their start right here. I'm speaking of White Castle (founded in Wichita in 1916) and Pizza Hut (started here in 1958).

"In the first half of the twentieth century, White Castle was the first company to create a different 'sense of place' widely accepted for selling hamburgers," a 1999 book called *Fast Food* noted. "No less a hamburger mogul than Ray Kroc, McDonald's legendary founder, recalled vividly that it was at a White Castle, serving its distinctive, one-inch-square meat patties, that he first learned about hamburgers eaten outside the home."

The same book goes on to call Pizza Hut "the company that initially popularized pizza as fast food." (No matter that Wichita no longer boasts a White Castle, and Pizza Hut's headquarters departed some years ago.)

Once branded as Fast-Food Capital of the Universe, the city could open a Fast-Food Museum and Hall of Fame. Think of it: a museum devoted to arguably the single biggest influence on life in the past fifty years. After all, if we are what we eat, then what has shaped us more than fast food? And I'm not talking just about waistlines.

According to statistics, Americans spent $239 billion on fast food in 2020—more than on higher education or new cars and more than on movies,

Above: The original Pizza Hut building is now a museum on the campus of Wichita State University. The author proposes a much grander museum celebrating the city's role in the fast-food industry. *Courtesy of the Original Pizza Hut museum.*

Right: A recipe for Pizza Hut sauce written on a napkin by co-founder Dan Carney is displayed at the museum. *Courtesy of the Original Pizza Hut museum.*

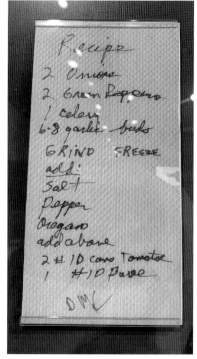

books, magazines, newspapers, videos and recorded music. Internationally, fast food might be our most influential export after music and athletic shoes.

The real beauty of the proposal is that it shouldn't cost the city a cent. Can you say corporate sponsorship? There could be a KFC Pavilion, Taco Bell Auditorium and Papa John's Visitors Center. McDonald's would have its own arched wing, or maybe two. If each fast-food chain devoted a mere 1 percent of its advertising to promoting the museum, everyone in the country would have heard of it within a week. The synergetic possibilities are truly staggering.

Inside the museum would be exhibits featuring the industry's greatest successes (the Whopper, Frosty and so on) and miscues (that Subway guy). There'd be hands-on exhibits, too, where the tiny percent of visitors who hadn't worked in a fast-food restaurant at one time or another in their lives could see what it's like flipping burgers.

Each year, food writers would nominate another fast-food icon to join Kroc, Harland Sanders, Wichita's own Carney brothers and other fast-food pioneers in the hall of fame.

Naturally, there'd be a food court. Make that the Mother of All Food Courts.

I see the Fast-Food Hall of Fame and Museum rising gaudily from the banks of the Arkansas River. You know, with columns shaped like giant French fries and a roof resembling a hamburger bun.

Maybe I'm having a little fun with the idea, but the more I think about it, the more sense it makes:

Wichita, Fast-Food Capital of the Universe.

THE HOLE-IN-THE-WALL GANG

Despite the generally positive take on Wichita's food scene that I've presented in these pages, there is one development that must be lamented: the demise of the hole-in-the-wall burger joint. Twenty years ago, they seemed to be everywhere, which meant you could get a freshly made burger hot off the grill for no more than you'd typically spend at McDonald's. All you had to do was not be in a hurry and not be too picky about the surroundings.

I'm talking about places like Burger Station up north, Charlie's on West 13th Street, Southern Style Foods at Ninth and Grove and the most famous of all, Takhoma Burger, originally located near what's now Riverfront Stadium. All now gone, along with at least a dozen of their burger brethren.

Hole-in-the-wall burger joints were easy to recognize, starting with a big bag of potatoes lying somewhere waiting to be turned into French fries. The owner would be there, both to cook your order and take your money. The grease in to-go orders would soak through the bag by the time you got to your car.

Other tip-offs included décor and seating, or rather the lack of them. Burger joints do not have more than a dozen seats. A rickety picnic table within close range of train tracks is a good sign.

Burger joints also do not sell chicken nuggets, salads and frozen yogurt, and they are not fast. Great burgers are made to order, and the burger cognoscenti know this.

Left: A double cheeseburger from Bomber Burger starts with one and a half pounds of beef.

Below: Bomber Burger draws burger fans from all over to south Wichita.

Through the years, my favorite came to be Jack's Coffee House on South Hydraulic, which wasn't owned by Jack and didn't serve coffee but did make a fantastic burger. The proprietor told me her secret was buying marked-down ground beef from a local supermarket—for the additional aging, perhaps?—and sprinkling a little pickle juice on the meat while it cooked. Despite numerous fans, it closed.

Fortunately, the city still boasts an establishment that sets a standard both for burgers and hole-in-the-wall joints: Bomber Burger on South Clifton. Owner Chris Rickard recently marked his twentieth year of serving up huge burgers—the current weight of a single is three-quarters of a pound—hand-cut fries, cold beverages and colorful commentary in a no-frills setting.

Bomber Burger routinely wins "best burger" awards on a local, regional and national basis. Plenty has been written about Rickard's obsession with quality (his blog handle is burgernazi) and politically incorrect banner. Suffice it to note that the sign outside reads: "Spangles can kiss our ass!"

On second thought, I can't resist telling the top three Rickard stories:

1. Rickard once paid a $1,000 health department fine with ten thousand dimes.
2. Rickard once chased down an unruly customer who'd assaulted another customer, holding him until police arrived despite having his throat sliced open with a broken beer mug.
3. Rickard once so enraged a female customer with an off-color (though very funny) remark that she sprayed down his restaurant with ketchup.

You don't see any of *that* at Applebee's.

Sport Burger on Hillside and Buster's on MacArthur are other burger joints that do a great job, but for the most part, it's a business model that seems on the way out. And as a result, the city has lost some of its sizzle.

Afterword

SUE CHEF GETS THE LAST WORD

A few years after joining me in Wichita, my wife started calling herself "Sue Chef." This is a reference to the subordinate role she supposedly takes in the kitchen. It's her contention that I get all the credit while she does the dirty work, much like a sous chef in a restaurant.

She's got a nickname for me, too—the Food God, generally used when something goes awry in the kitchen. As in: "Betcha the Food God didn't mean to burn that."

Naturally, I couldn't resist writing about Sue Chef in the *Wichita Eagle*. Readers seemed to enjoy tales of her adventures with food.

There was the time she mishandled a particularly spicy jalapeño and found herself standing in the shower, fully clothed, rinsing out her eyes while girlfriends called 911. And the time she destroyed our mixer trying to make cheesecake with unsoftened cream cheese. I might have mentioned her occasional struggles with kitchen math ("Honey, how many tablespoons are in a pound?").

But I also paid tribute to her adventurous, fun-loving spirit. This is a woman who ate fried ant eggs and worms on our honeymoon in Puerto Vallarta because I'd heard of a place that served world-class versions of them. She has gamely tried every bizarre dish I've prepared, from braised duck tongues to cold squid salad. If one of these experiments turns out really good, we say it's "company ready." At the other end of the spectrum is "pizza night," when things go horribly, into-the-trashcan wrong.

Sue Chef in a contemplative mood. *Photo by Jaime Green.*

When I suggested we get chickens for the fresh eggs they'd provide, she was initially resistant, claiming she'd be allergic. They are now the most pampered and fussed-over flock of birds west of the Mississippi.

We agree on most things related to food. For instance, we agree that dinner guests should arrive five to fifteen minutes late (but no later), preferably with wine bottle in hand.

If I'm occasionally bossy in the kitchen, it's because Sue is in charge of the other 80 percent of our house and lives. She also lets me mow the lawn.

The truth is, Sue is a fabulous cook, but she knows it means more to me. She's the one who gets guests to our home, creates a welcoming environment and makes sure they have a good time.

As for when it's just us, I realized a long time ago that cooking for two is a lot more fun than cooking for one. For all these reasons, I give Sue Chef the last word and recipe.

The word is one of her favorites: enjoy!

*Sue Chef's Semi-Famous Beer-Butt Chicken

1 chicken, 4–5 pounds

Rub:
2 tablespoons Cajun or Creole seasoning
1 tablespoon kosher salt
1 teaspoon ground sage
1 teaspoon chili powder
1 teaspoon oregano
1 teaspoon cayenne pepper
6 cloves garlic, minced
1 bunch cilantro, chopped

1 12-ounce can beer, about half full

Sauce:

1 cup grape jelly
1 cup ketchup
¼ cup Worcestershire sauce

Rinse and dry chicken; remove giblets if present.

For the rub, pile all the ingredients on a cutting board and run over them with a chef's knife until a paste is formed. Apply rub mixture all over chicken. If desired, loosen the skin covering the breast and leg quarters by working your fingers under it, then spread some rub there as well.

Preheat grill to 350 degrees by lighting coals or burners on one side of grill. Place chicken on opposite side of grill; position the chicken's cavity over a 12-ounce can of beer and spread its legs out to keep it from falling. Close grill and cook for about 1½ hours or until fully cooked, rotating chicken once. When done, juices from chicken will run clear and legs will move easily in their joints. Near end of cooking time, baste with some of the sauce; serve remaining sauce with the chicken.

SOURCES

I consulted two sources while writing the chapters on Lebanese and Mexican food in Wichita: *Wichita's Lebanese Heritage* by Jay M. Price, Victoria Sherry and Matthew Namee (The History Press, 2010) and a history of the city's North End compiled by students in Wichita State University's public history class.

Many of the book's recipes were previously published as part of articles I wrote for the *Wichita Eagle*, *Splurge* magazine or *The Active Age* and are used here by permission. Others were given to me during the writing of this book. I have noted where recipes also appear in cookbooks by other authors.

I consulted articles in the *Wichita Eagle* by Denise Neil and Carrie Rengers while writing the chapter on restaurant recipes. Photographs are by the author unless otherwise noted.

RECIPE INDEX

MAIN DISHES

RECIPE INDEX

SIDE DISHES

DESSERTS

DRINKS

OTHER

ABOUT THE AUTHOR

Joe Stumpe is a writer, musician and culinary instructor. His first book, *Wicked Wichita*, was published by The History Press in 2018.